THE
LOST
DIMENSION

PAUL VIRILIO

THE
LOST
DIMENSION

Translated by Daniel Moshenberg

SEMIOTEXT(E)

Semiotext(e) books are published by
Autonomedia
55 South Eleventh Street
POB 568 Williamsburgh Station
Brooklyn, New York 11211 USA
(718) 387-6471

Special thanks to Sue Ann Harkey, Daniel Moshenberg,
Paul Virilio and Jordan Zinovich.

This book was first published as
L'espace critique, (Paris: Christian Bourgois, 1984).

Printed in the United States of America.

TABLE OF CONTENTS

THE
LOST
DIMENSION

1

The Overexposed City

At the beginning of the 60's, with black ghettoes rioting, the mayor of Philadelphia announced: "From here on in, the frontiers of the State pass to the interior of the cities." While this sentence translated the political reality for all Americans who were being discriminated against, it also pointed to an even larger dimension, given the construction of the Berlin Wall, on August 13, 1961, in the heart of the ancient capital of the Reich.

Since then, this assertion has been confirmed time and again: Belfast, Londonderry where not so long ago certain streets bore a yellow band separating the Catholic side from the Protestant, so that neither would move too far, leaving a chainlink no man's land to divide their communities even more clearly. And then there's Beirut with its East and West sections, its tortured internal boundaries, its tunnels and its mined boulevards.

Basically, the American mayor's statement revealed a general phenomenon that was just beginning to hit the

9

capital cities as well as the provincial towns and hamlets, the phenomenon of obligatory introversion in which the City sustained the first effects of a multinational economy modelled along the lines of industrial enterprises, a real urban redeployment which soon contributed to the gutting of certain worker cities such as Liverpool and Sheffield in England, Detroit and Saint Louis in the United States, Dortmund in West Germany, and all of this at the very moment in which other areas were being built up, around tremendous international airports, a METROPLEX, a metropolitan complex such as Dallas / Fort Worth. Since the 70's and the beginnings of the world economic crisis, the construction of these airports was further subjected to the imperatives of the defense against air pirates.

Construction no longer derived simply from traditional technical constraint. The plan had become a function of the risks of "terrorist contamination" and the disposition of sites conceived of as sterile zones for departures and non-sterile zones for arrivals. Suddenly, all forms of loading and unloading — regardless of passenger, baggage, or freight status — and all manner of airport transit had to be submitted to a system of interior / exterior traffic control. The architecture that resulted from this had little to do with the architect's personality. It emerged instead from perceived public security requirements.

As the last gateway to the State, the airport came to resemble the fort, port or railway station of earlier days. As airports were turned into theaters of necessary regulation of exchange and communication, they also became breeding and testing grounds for high-pressured experiments in control and aerial surveillance performed for and by a new "air and border patrol," whose anti-terrorist exploits began to make headlines with the intervention of the German GS.G9 border guards in the Mogadishu hijacking, several thousand miles away from Germany.

The Overexposed City

At that instant, the strategy of confining the sick or the suspect gave way to a tactic of mid-voyage interception. Practically, this meant examining clothing and baggage, which explains the sudden proliferation of cameras, radars and detectors in all restricted passageways. When the French built "maximum security cell-blocks," they used the magnetized doorways that airports had had for years. Paradoxically, the equipment that ensured maximal freedom in travel formed part of the core of penitentiary incarceration. At the same time, in a number of residential areas in the United States, security was maintained exclusively through closed-circuit television hook-ups with a central police station. In banks, in supermarkets, and on major highways, where tollbooths resembled the ancient city gates, the rite of passage was no longer intermittent. It had become immanent.

In this new perspective devoid of horizon, the city was entered not through a gate nor through an *arc de triomphe*, but rather through an electronic audience system. Users of the road were no longer understood to be inhabitants or privileged residents. They were now interlocutors in permanent transit. From this moment on, continuity no longer breaks down in space, not in the physical space of urban lots nor in the juridical space of their property tax records. From here, continuity is ruptured in time, in a time that advanced technologies and industrial redeployment incessantly arrange through a series of interruptions, such as plant closings, unemployment, casual labor, and successive or simultaneous disappearing acts. These serve to organize and then disorganize the urban environment to the point of provoking the irreversible decay and degradation of neighborhoods, as in the housing development near Lyon where the occupants' "rate of rotation" became so great — people staying for a year and then moving on — that it contributed to the ruin of a place that each inhabitant found adequate . . .

☙ ☙ ☙

In fact, since the originary enclosures, the concept of boundary has undergone numerous changes as regards both the facade and the neighborhood it fronts. From the palisade to the screen, by way of stone ramparts, the boundary–surface has recorded innumerable perceptible and imperceptible transformations, of which the latest is probably that of the interface. Once again, we have to approach the question of access to the City in a new manner. For example, does the metropolis possess its own facade? At which moment does the city show us its face?

The phrase "to go into town," which replaced the nineteenth century's "to go to town," indicates the uncertainty of the encounter, as if we could no longer stand before the city but rather abide forever within. If the metropolis is still a place, a geographic site, it no longer has anything to do with the classical oppositions of city / country nor center / periphery. The city is no longer organized into a localized and axial estate. While the suburbs contributed to this dissolution, in fact the intramural–extramural opposition collapsed with the transport revolutions and the development of communication and telecommunications technologies. These promoted the merger of disconnected metropolitan fringes into a single urban mass.

In effect, we are witnessing a paradoxical moment in which the opacity of building materials is reduced to zero. With the invention of the steel skeleton construction, curtain walls made of light and transparent materials, such as glass or plastics, replace stone facades, just as tracing paper, acetate and plexiglass replace the opacity of paper in the designing phase.

On the other hand, with the screen interface of computers, television and teleconferences, the surface of inscription, hitherto devoid of depth, becomes a kind of "distance," a depth of field of a new kind of representation, a visibility without any face-to-face encounter in which the *vis-à-vis* of the ancient streets disappears and is erased. In this situation, a difference of position blurs into fusion and confusion. Deprived of objective boundaries, the architectonic element begins to drift and float in an electronic ether, devoid of spatial dimensions, but inscribed in the singular temporality of an instantaneous diffusion. From here on, people can't be separated by physical obstacles or by temporal distances. With the interfacing of computer terminals and video monitors, distinctions of *here* and *there* no longer mean anything.

This sudden reversion of boundaries and oppositions introduces into everyday, common space an element which until now was reserved for the world of microscopes. There is no *plenum*; space is not filled with matter. Instead, an unbounded expanse appears in the false perspective of the machines' luminous emissions. From here on, constructed space occurs within an electronic topology where the framing of perspective and the gridwork weft of numerical images renovate the division of urban property. The ancient private / public occultation and the distinction between housing and traffic are replaced by an overexposure in which the difference between "near" and "far" simply ceases to exist, just as the difference between "micro" and "macro" vanished in the scanning of the electron microscope.

The representation of the modern city can no longer depend on the ceremonial opening of gates, nor on the ritual processions and parades lining the streets and avenues with spectators. From here on, urban architecture has to work with the opening of a new "technological space-time." In terms of access, telematics replaces the doorway. The sound of gates gives way to the clatter of data banks and the rites of passage of a technical culture whose progress is disguised by the immateriality of its parts and networks. Instead of operating in the space of a constructed social fabric, the intersecting and connecting grid of highway and service systems now occurs in the sequences of an imperceptible organization of time in which the man / machine interface replaces the facades of buildings as the surfaces of property allotments.

⊛   ⊛   ⊛

Where once the opening of the city gates announced the alternating progression of days and nights, now we awaken to the opening of shutters and televisions. The day has been changed. A new day has been added to the astronomers' solar day, to the flickering day of candles, to the electric light. It is an electronic false-day, and it appears on a calendar of information "commutations" that has absolutely no relationship whatsoever to real time. Chronological and historical time, time that passes, is replaced by a time that exposes itself instantaneously. On the computer screen, a time period becomes the "support-surface" of inscription. Literally, or better cinematically, time surfaces. Thanks to the cathode-ray tube, spatial dimensions have become inseparable from their rate of transmission. As a unity of place without any unity of time, the City has disappeared into the heterogeneity of that regime comprised of the temporality of advanced technologies. The urban figure is no longer designated by a dividing line that separates here from there. Instead, it has become a computerized timetable.

Where once one necessarily entered the city by means of a physical gateway, now one passes through an audiovisual protocol in which the methods of audience and surveillance have transformed even the forms of public greeting and daily reception. Within this place of optical illusion, in which the people occupy transportation and transmission time instead of inhabiting space, inertia tends to renovate an old sedentariness, which results in the persistence of urban sites. With the new instantaneous communications media, arrival supplants departure: without necessarily leaving, everything "arrives."

Until recently, the city separated its "intramural" population from those outside the walls. Today, people are divided according to aspects of time. Where once an entire "downtown" area indicated a long historical period, now only a few monuments will do. Further, the new technological time has no relation to any calendar of events nor to any collective memory. It is pure computer time, and as such helps construct a permanent present, an unbounded, timeless intensity that is destroying the tempo of a progressively degraded society.

What is a monument within this regime? Instead of an intricately wrought portico or a monumental walk punctuated by sumptuous buildings, we now have idleness and monumental waiting for service from a machine. Everyone is busily waiting in front of some communications or telecommunications apparatus, lining up at tollbooths, poring over captains' checklists, sleeping with computer consoles on their nightstands. Finally, the gateway is turned into a conveyance of vehicles and vectors whose disruption creates less a space than a countdown, in which work occupies the center of time while uncontrolled time of vacations and unemployment form a periphery, the suburbs of time, a clearing away of activities in which each person is exiled to a life of privacy and deprivation.

If, despite the wishes of postmodern architects, the city from here on is deprived of gateway entries, it is because the urban wall has long been breached by an infinitude of openings and ruptured enclosures. While less apparent than those of antiquity, these are equally effective, constraining and segregating. The illusion of the industrial revolution in transportation misled us as to the limitlessness of progress. Industrial time-management has imperceptibly compensated for the loss of rural territories. In the nineteenth century, the city / country attraction emptied agrarian space of its cultural and social substance. At the end of the twentieth century, urban space loses its geopolitical reality to the exclusive benefit of systems of instantaneous deportation whose technological intensity ceaselessly upsets all of our social structures. These systems include the deportation of people in the redeployment of modes of production, the deportation of attention, of the human face-to-face and the urban *vis-à-vis* encounters at the level of human / machine interaction. In effect, all of this participates in a new "post-urban" and transnational kind of concentration, as indicated by a number of recent events.

Despite the rising cost of energy, the American middle classes are evacuating the cities of the East. Following the transformation of inner cities into ghettoes and slums, we now are watching the deterioration of the cities as regional centers. From Washington to Chicago, from Boston to Saint Louis, the major urban centers are shrinking. On the brink of bankruptcy, New York City lost ten percent of its population in the last ten years. Meanwhile, Detroit lost twenty percent of its inhabitants, Cleveland 23 percent, Saint Louis 27 percent. Already, whole neighborhoods have turned into ghost towns.

These harbingers of an imminent "post-industrial" deurbanization promise an exodus that will affect all of the developed countries. Predicted for the last forty years, this deregulation of the management of space comes from an economic and political illusion about the persistence of sites constructed in the era of automotive management of time, and in the epoch of the development of audiovisual technologies of retinal persistence.

⊛ ⊛ ⊛

"Each surface is an interface between two environments that is ruled by a constant activity in the form of an exchange between the two substances placed in contact with one another."

This new scientific definition of surface demonstrates the contamination at work: the "boundary, or limiting surface" has turned into an osmotic membrane, like a blotting pad. Even if this last definition is more rigorous than earlier ones, it still signals a change in the notion of limitation. The limitation of space has become commutation: the radical separation, the necessary crossing, the transit of a constant activity, the activity of incessant exchanges, the transfer between two environments and two substances. What used to be the boundary of a material, its "terminus," has become an entryway hidden in the most imperceptible entity. From here on, the appearance of surfaces and superficies conceals a secret transparency, a thickness without thickness, a volume without volume, an imperceptible quantity.

If this situation corresponds with the physical reality of the infinitesimally small, it also fits that of the infinitely large. When what was visibly nothing becomes "something," the greatest distance no longer precludes perception. The greatest geophysical expanse contracts as it becomes more concentrated. In the interface of the screen, everything is always already there, offered to view in the immediacy of an instantaneous transmission. In 1980, for example, when Ted Turner decided to launch Cable News Network as a round-the-clock live news station, he transformed his subscribers' living space into a kind of global broadcast studio for world events.

Thanks to satellites, the cathode-ray window brings to each viewer the light of another day and the presence of the antipodal place. If space is that which keeps everything from occupying the same place, this abrupt confinement brings absolutely everything precisely to that "place," that location that has no location. The exhaustion of physical, or natural, relief and of temporal distances telescopes all localization and all position. As with live televised events, the places become interchangeable at will.

The instantaneity of ubiquity results in the atopia of a singular interface. After the spatial and temporal distances, *speed distance* obliterates the notion of physical dimension. Speed suddenly becomes a primal dimension that defies all temporal and physical measurements. This radical erasure is equivalent to a momentary inertia in the environment. The old agglomeration disappears in the intense acceleration of telecommunications, in order to give rise to a new type of concentration: the concentration of a domiciliation without domiciles, in which property boundaries, walls and fences no longer signify the permanent physical obstacle. Instead, they now form an interruption of an emission or of an electronic shadow zone which repeats the play of daylight and the shadow of buildings.

A strange topology is hidden in the obviousness of televised images. Architectural plans are displaced by the sequence plans of an invisible montage. Where geographical space once was arranged according to the geometry of an apparatus of rural or urban boundary setting, time is now organized according to imperceptible fragmentations of the technical time span, in which the cutting, as of a momentary interruption, replaces the lasting disappearance, the "program guide" replaces the chain link fence, just as the railroads' timetables once replaced the almanacs.

"The camera has become our best inspector," declared John F. Kennedy, a little before being struck down in a Dallas street. Effectively, the camera allows us to participate in certain political and optical events. Consider, for example, the irruption phenomenon, in which the City allows itself to be seen thoroughly and completely, or the diffraction phenomenon, in which its image reverberates beyond the atmosphere to the farthest reaches of space, while the endoscope and the scanner allow us to see to the farthest reaches of life.

This overexposure attracts our attention to the extent that it offers a world without antipodes and without hidden aspects, a world in which opacity is but a momentary interlude. Note how the illusion of proximity barely lasts. Where once the *polis* inaugurated a political theater, with its *agora* and its *forum,* now there is only a cathode-ray screen, where the shadows and spectres of a community dance amid their processes of disappearance, where cinematism broadcasts the last appearance of urbanism, the last image of an urbanism without urbanity. This is where tact and contact give way to televisual impact. While tele-conferencing allows long-distance conferences with the advantage derived from the absence of displacement, tele-negotiating inversely allows for the production of distance in discussions, even when the members of the conversation are right next to each other. This is a little like those telephone crazies for whom the receiver induces flights of verbal fancy amid the anonymity of a remote control aggressiveness.

⊛   ⊛   ⊛

Where does the city without gates begin? Probably inside that fugitive anxiety, that shudder that seizes the minds of those who, just returning from a long vacation, contemplate the imminent encounter with mounds of unwanted mail or with a house that's been broken into and emptied of its contents. It begins with the urge to flee and escape for a second from an oppressive technological environment, to regain one's senses and one's sense of self. While spatial escape may be possible, temporal escape is not. Unless we think of lay-offs as "escape hatches," the ultimate form of paid vacation, the forward flight responds to a post-industrial illusion whose ill effects we are just beginning to feel. Already, the theory of "job sharing" introduced to a new segment of the community — offering each person an alternative in which sharing work-time could easily lead to a whole new sharing of space as well — mirrors the rule of an endless periphery in which the homeland and the colonial settlement would replace the industrial city and its suburbs. Consider, for example, the Community Development Project, which promotes the proliferation of local development projects based on community forces, and which is intended to reincorporate the English inner cities.

Where does the edge of the exo-city begin? Where can we find the gate without a city? Probably in the new American technologies of instantaneous destruction (with explosives) of tall buildings and in the politics of systematic destruction of housing projects suddenly deemed as "unfit for the new French way of life, as in Venissieux, La Courneuve or Gagny. According to a recent French study, released by the Association for Community Development, "The destruction of 300,000 residential units over a five-year period would cost 10 billion francs per year, while creating 100,000 new jobs. In addition, at the end of the demolition / reconstruction, the fiscal receipts would be 6 to 10 billion francs above the sum of public moneys invested."

One final question arises here. In a period of economic crisis, will mass destruction of the large cities replace the traditional politics of large public works? If that happens, there will be no essential difference between economic-industrial recession and war.

⍺ ⍺ ⍺

Architecture or post-architecture? Ultimately, the intellectual debate surrounding modernity seems part of a de-realization phenomenon which simultaneously involves disciplines of expression, modes of representation and modes of communication. The current wave of explosive debates within the media concerning specific political acts and their social communication now also involves the architectural expression, which cannot be removed from the world of communication systems, to the precise extent that it suffers the direct or indirect fall-out of various "means of communication," such as the automobile or audiovisual systems.

Basically, along with construction techniques, there's always the construction *of* techniques, that collection of spatial and temporal mutations that is constantly reorganizing both the world of everyday experience and the esthetic representations of contemporary life. Constructed space, then, is more than simply the concrete and material substance of constructed structures, the permanence of elements and the architectonics of urbanistic details. It also exists as the sudden proliferation and the incessant multiplication of special effects which, along with the consciousness of time and of distances, affect the perception of the environment.

This technological deregulation of various milieus is also topological to the exact extent that — instead of constructing a perceptible and visible chaos, such as the processes of degradation or destruction implied in accident, aging and war — it inversely and paradoxically builds an imperceptible order, which is invisible but just as practical as masonry or the public highways system. In all likelihood, the essence of what we insist on calling urbanism is composed / decomposed by these transfer, transit and transmission systems, these transport and transmigration networks whose immaterial configuration reiterates the cadastral organization and the building of monuments.

If there are any monuments today, they are certainly not of the visible order, despite the twists and turns of architectural excess. No longer part of the order of perceptible appearances nor of the esthetic of the apparition of volumes assembled under the sun, this monumental disproportion now resides within the obscure luminescence of terminals, consoles and other electronic night-stands. Architecture is more than an array of techniques designed to shelter us from the storm. It is an instrument of measure, a sum total of knowledge that, contending with the natural environment, becomes capable of organizing society's time and space. This geodesic capacity to define a unity of time and place for all actions now enters into direct conflict with the structural capacities of the means of mass communication.

Two procedures confront each other. The first is primarily material, constructed of physical elements, walls, thresholds and levels, all precisely located. The other is immaterial, and hence its representations, images and messages afford neither locale nor stability, since they are the vectors of a momentary, instantaneous expression, with all the manipulated meanings and misinformation that presupposes.

The first one is architectonic and urbanistic in that it organizes and constructs durable geographic and political space. The second haphazardly arranges and deranges space-time, the continuum of societies. The point here is not to propose a Manichaean judgment that opposes the physical to the metaphysical, but rather to attempt to catch the status of contemporary, and particularly urban, architecture within the disconcerting concert of advanced technologies. If architectonics developed with the rise of the City and the discovery and colonization of emerging lands, since the conclusion of that conquest, architecture, like the large cities, has rapidly declined. While continuing to invest in internal technical equipment, architecture has become progressively introverted, becoming a kind of machinery gallery, a museum of sciences and technologies, technologies derived from industrial *machinism,* from the transportation revolution and from so-called "conquest of space." So it makes perfect sense that when we discuss space technologies today, we are not referring to architecture but rather to the engineering that launches us into outer space.

All of this occurs as if architectonics had been merely a subsidiary technology, surpassed by other technologies that produced accelerated displacement and sidereal projection. In fact, this is a question of the nature of architectural performance, of the telluric function of the constructed realm and the relationships between a certain cultural technology and the earth. The development of the City as the conservatory of classical technologies has already contributed to the proliferation of architecture through its projection into every spatial direction, with the demographic concentration and the extreme vertical densification of the urban milieu, in direct opposition to the agrarian model. The advanced technologies have since continued to prolong this "advance," through the thoughtless and all-encompassing expansion of the architectonic, especially with the rise of the means of transportation.

Right now, vanguard technologies, derived from the military conquest of space, are already launching homes, and perhaps tomorrow the City itself, into planetary orbit. With inhabited satellites, space shuttles and space stations as floating laboratories of high-tech research and industry, architecture is flying high, with curious repercussions for the fate of post-industrial societies, in which the cultural markers tend to disappear progressively, what with the decline of the arts and the slow regression of the primary technologies.

Is urban architecture becoming an outmoded technology, as happened to extensive agriculture, from which came the debacles of megalopolis? Will architectonics become simply another decadent form of dominating the earth, with results like those of the uncontrolled exploitation of primary resources? Hasn't the decrease in the number of major cities already become the trope for industrial decline and forced unemployment, symbolizing the failure of scientific materialism?

The recourse to History proposed by experts of postmodernity is a cheap trick that allows them to avoid the question of Time, the regime of trans-historical temporality derived from technological ecosystems. If in fact there is a crisis today, it is a crisis of ethical and esthetic references, the inability to come to terms with events in an environment where the appearances are against us. With the growing imbalance between direct and indirect information that comes of the development of various means of communication, and its tendency to privilege information mediated to the detriment of meaning, it seems that the *reality effect* replaces immediate reality. Lyotard's modern crisis of grand narratives betrays the effect of new technologies, with the accent, from here on, placed on means more than ends.

The grand narratives of theoretical causality were thus displaced by the petty narratives of practical opportunity, and, finally, by the micro-narratives of autonomy. At issue here is no longer the "crisis of modernity," the progressive deterioration of commonly held ideals, the proto-foundation of the meaning of History, to the benefit of more-or-less restrained narratives connected to the autonomous development of individuals. The problem now is with the narrative itself, with an official discourse or mode of representation, connected until now with the universally recognized capacity to say, describe and inscribe reality. This is the heritage of the Renaissance. Thus, the crisis in the conceptualization of "narrative" appears as the other side of the crisis of the conceptualization of "dimension" as geometrical narrative, the discourse of measurement of a reality visibly offered to all.

The crisis of the grand narrative that gives rise to the micro-narrative finally becomes the crisis of the narrative of the grand and the petty.

The Overexposed City

This marks the advent of a disinformation in which excess and incommensurability are, for "post-modernity," what the philosophical resolution of problems and the resolution of the pictorial and architectural image were to the birth of the "enlightenment."

The crisis in the conceptualization of dimension becomes the crisis of the whole.

In other words, the substantial, homogeneous space derived from classical Greek geometry gives way to an accidental, heterogeneous space in which sections and fractions become essential once more. Just as the land suffered the mechanization of agriculture, urban topography has continuously paid the price for the atomization and disintegration of surfaces and of all references that tend towards all kinds of transmigrations and transformations. This sudden exploding of whole forms, this destruction of the properties of the individual by industrialization, is felt less in the city's space — despite the dissolution of the suburbs — than in the time — understood as sequential perceptions — of urban appearances. In fact, transparency has long supplanted appearances. Since the beginning of the twentieth century, the classical depth of field has been revitalized by the depth of time of advanced technologies. Both the film and aeronautics industries took off soon after the ground was broken for the grand boulevards. The parades on Haussmann Boulevard gave way to the Lumière brothers' accelerated motion picture inventions; the esplanades of Les Invalides gave way to the invalidation of the city plan. The screen abruptly became the city square, the crossroads of all mass media.

From the esthetics of the appearance of a *stable* image — present as an aspect of its static nature — to the esthetics of the *dis*appearance of an *unstable* image — present in its cinematic and cinematographic flight of escape — we have witnessed a transmutation of representations. The emergence of forms as volumes destined to persist as long as their materials would allow has given way to images whose duration is purely retinal. So, more than Venturi's Las Vegas, it is Hollywood that merits urbanist scholarship, for, after the theater-cities of Antiquity and of the Italian Renaissance, it was Hollywood that was the first Cinecittà, the city of living cinema where stage-sets and reality, tax-plans and scripts, the living and the living dead, mix and merge deliriously.

Here more than anywhere else advanced technologies combined to form a synthetic space-time.

Babylon of filmic de-formation, industrial zone of pretense, Hollywood was built neighborhood by neighborhood, block by block, on the twilight of appearances, the success of magicians' tricks, the rise of epic productions like those of D. W. Griffith, all the while waiting for the megalomaniacal urbanizations of Disneyland, Disney World and Epcot Center. When Francis Ford Coppola, in *One From the Heart*, electronically inlaid his actors into a life-size Las Vegas built at the Zoetrope studios in Hollywood (simply because the director wanted the city to adapt to his shooting schedule instead of the other way around), he overpowered Venturi, not by demonstrating the ambiguities of contemporary architecture, but by showing the "spectral" characters of the city and its denizens.

The utopian "architecture on paper" of the 1960's took on the video-electronic special effects of people like Harryhausen and Tumbull, just at the precise instant that computer screens started popping up in architectural firms. "Video doesn't mean I see; it means I fly," according to Nam June Paik. With this technology, the "aerial view" no longer involves the theoretical altitudes of scale models. It has become an opto-electronic interface operating in real time, with all that this implies for the redefinition of the image. If aviation — appearing the same year as cinematography — entailed a revision of point of view and a radical mutation of our perception of the world, infographic technologies will likewise force a readjustment of reality and its representations. We already see this in "Tactical Mapping Systems," a videodisk produced by the United States Defense Department's Agency for Advanced Research Projects. This system offers a continuous view of Aspen, Colorado, by accelerating or decelerating the speed of 54,000 images, changing direction or season as easily as one switches television channels, turning the town into a kind of shooting gallery in which the functions of eyesight and weaponry melt into each other.

If architectonics once measured itself according to geology, according to the tectonics of natural reliefs, with pyramids, towers and other neo-gothic tricks, today it measures itself according to state-of-the-art technologies, whose vertiginous prowess exiles all of us from the terrestrial horizon.

Neo-geological, the "Monument Valley" of some pseudo-lithic era, today's metropolis is a phantom landscape, the fossil of past societies whose technologies were intimately aligned with the visible transformation of matter, a project from which the sciences have increasingly turned away.

2
The Morphological Irruption

"In politics, unlike physics, perceptions are facts," wrote Lionel S. Johns, adjunct-director of the Office of Technology Assessment of the U. S. Senate. Who today would deny that the *polis,* having donated its etymology to the word politics, is part of the domain of the facts of perception? If we find that we can now easily imagine the disappearance of cities, in both anti-city nuclear strategies and post-industrial redeployment plans, it is because for the last forty years the figure of the city has been dissipated and withered down to a nub, until finally it has become a memory, a recollection of the unity that was a neighborhood, a unity that has continuously suffered the fall-out of the mutations of the means of mass communications, waiting to disappear in the post-industrial exodus, the exile of structural unemployment brought on by robotization and the supreme rule of transport machines.

THE LOST DIMENSION

Today, the abolition of distances in time by various means of communications and telecommunications results in a confusion in which the image of the City suffers the direct and indirect effects of iconological torsion and distortion, in which the most elementary reference points disappear one by one. With the decay of urban centrality and axiality, the symbolic and historic reference points go first. Then, when the industrial apparatus and the monuments lose their meanings, the architectonic references vanish. Most decisively, the demise of the ancient categorization and partition of the physical dimension leads to the loss of the geometric reference points.

The recuperated supremacy of distance-speed, measured as mach, bit-second, nano-second, over that of space, in kilometers, or time, in km/h, restores that "primitive grandeur," the privileged vector of pre-geometric organizations of space, and thereby contributes to the dissolution of the traditional formation of appearances. The communal perception of sensible space was a formation based since Antiquity on the mnemotechnic merits of Euclidean geometry, a geometry of regular plane surfaces regulated by a system of dimensions that dissects a universe in which the measure of superficies dominated the geographic, the urban and rural cadastral, and the architectonic partitioning of constructed elements. Today, on the other hand, the world-view based on orthogonal orthodoxy has given way to a new perception, in which the very concept of physical dimension has progressively lost its meaning and analytical power as a form of dissecting or dismounting perceptive reality. Instead we find other, electronic means of evaluating space and time, ones which share no common ground with the measuring systems of the past.

From now on, we are directly or indirectly witnessing a co-production of sensible reality, in which direct and mediated perceptions merge into an instantaneous representation

The Morphological Irruption

of space and the surrounding environment. The great divide — between the reality of temporal and spatial distances and the distancing of various video-graphic and info-graphic representations — has ended. The direct observation of visible phenomena gives way to a tele-observation in which the observer has no immediate contact with the observed reality. While this sudden distancing admittedly offers the possibility of embracing hitherto unimaginably vast geographic and planetary expanses, it is also risky, in that the absence of any immediate perception of concrete reality produces a terrible imbalance between the sensible and the intelligible, one which can only result in errors of interpretation, errors all the more fatal, since the means of tele-detection and tele-communication are performers or, more precisely, video-performers.

In the face of this disordering of appearances, the orientation of point of view is not so much the angulation of surfaces and superficies of non-Euclidean geometry as it is the absence of any delay in the broadcast and rebroadcast of televised images. Thus, the primitive grandeur of speed-vector reassumes its importance in the redefinition of sensible space: the depth of *time* of opto-electronic teleology displaces the old depth of *field* of topology.

Point of view, the omnipresent center of the ancient perspective design, gives way to the televised instantaneity of a prospective observation, of a glance that pierces through the appearances of the greatest distances and the widest expanses. In this most recent experience of space that upsets the order of the visible that began in the Quattrocento, we are directly or indirectly witnessing a kind of tele-conquest of appearances that prolongs the telescope-effect of the Galilean plan. Irrespective of the vector of the spatial conquest (such as ship, submarine, airplane, spaceship, observation satellite), the observation machine is not so much the vehicle or apparatus of the physical displacement of observers, but

31

rather of an image. It is first of all a televised image. Basically, this becomes the one and only vector that works against transport engineering.

Irrespective of their motor performance, the new vehicles today are always surpassed by the "video-performance" of the transmission of images, and by the instantaneous representation of facts. Examples include the ultra-rapid camera producing a million images per second, the tele-detection camera, the super-high-resolution camera of the spy satellites, infra-red thermography, and radar-image technology.

Suddenly, we possess this ease of passing without transition or delay from the perception of the infinitesimally small to the perception of the infinitely large, from the immediate proximity of the visible to the visibility of all that lingers beyond our field of vision. And suddenly the ancient distinctions among the dimensions disappear. The dimensional dissection of classical geometry — where the point cut the line, and the line cut the plane, which then cut through the solids — has lost a critical part of its practical utility.

When transparency becomes manifest, it becomes a manifesto that re-organizes appearance and the measure of the sensible world and thus, almost immediately, its figure and its image-form.

The last "dissection" is not so much a fact of physical dimensions as it is a fact of the selection of speeds of perception and of representation, slowed down or sped up, that cut up the depth of time, the only temporal dimension. As such, the televised transparency replaces the appearance of direct vision. The sensible appearance of objects submits to the transmutation of the tele-observation and tele-communication of the facts of the image, as a globalizing image, that definitively displaces immediate perceptions, with all the implied risks of iconological disruptions. The synoptic homogeneity that results from the geometry of the point of view, much the same as the multi-temporal character of recorded facts, abolished the descriptive approach that so often prevails in scientific work in favor of a quantitative perception that has participated in a manner thoroughly opposed to statistical analysis. What becomes noteworthy, then, is the recuperated importance of the point in the electronic image, as if the 0 dimension suddenly retrieved its numerical significance, at the expense of the line, plane and solid — obsolete analogical dimensions all.

As the aerial photographic cartography of the IGN oversees French territories as a succession of 1100 rectangles — each one subdivided into 40 rectangles — satellite tele-detection relies on a unit of measurement — the pixel, a micro-element of the image — that corresponds somewhat to the photographic dot. "Thus, each image taken by the Landsat tele-detection satellite, covering a surface of 185 x 185 km, is composed of 7,581,000 pixels, each representing half a hectare. Each pixel is affected by four bits in the multispectral scanning system (MSS), which finally adds up to 30,324,000 bits. Thus, three successive satellite orbits provides more than 90 million bits. Since each pixel can be examined in relationship with its eight immediate neighbors, the treatment of a single limited expanse of 185 x 185 km can result in the consideration of hundreds of millions of bits of information."[1]

Given this explosion of data and its required information technology, the gap between the sensible and the intelligible continues to deepen. The same situation arises with the definition of television images projected on the traditional cathode ray screen of 625 lines. Each image is made up of some 400,000 points or 'discrete elements' (1,000,000 per 819 lines). With special effects and the wizardry of numerical electronics, each one of these elements is assigned a particular value. In what is called the grid memory, this allows for the continuous or discontinuous distortions and the partial or complete dislocations of the image obtained in this manner. The most recent investigations into the flat-front TV screen — slotted for wide distribution, thanks to the complementary aspects of its possibilities for both large-screen maximization and pocket miniaturization — turns on these problems of the quality of the image. The qualities of this opto-electronic placarding stem from the scanning system used: mechanical scanning of the image, at the beginning of television in 1930; electronic scanning of the traditional cathode-ray screen; opto-electronic auto-scanning of the 1960–70 plasma screens; and finally, of late, fluorescent screens, in which electronic scanning vanished, since it required as many electron sources as image-dots.

We find in satellite tele-detection, just as in the constitution of television images, the same electronic scanning, be it of landscape or of image. It is as if the fusion / confusion of the infinitely large and the infinitesimally small sprang from the deterioration of physical dimensions and analogical representations of space, and to the solitary benefit of numerical representation or, better, digital placarding. It is as if this fusion / confusion sprang from the too-great profusion of facts that occurs in the act of instantaneous representation.

At this point depth of *space* — understood as depth of the field of surfaces available to direct observation — vanishes, and is replaced by the depth of *time* of the *in*direct recording of numerical data. Whether the pixel corresponds to the luminous point of the synthetic image of the computer-enhanced conception, or whether, in the multispectral scanning of the spy-satellite, it represents a half-hectare of land, it demonstrates the same indifference, to the landscape, as actual, or as the simulated stretch of represented surfaces. Whether we speak of an enhanced drawing surface or of tele-detected superficies, in the end, all that counts is the quilt of numbered images and the instantaneity of their point by point re-transmission. At this stage, line, surface, and volume are merely aspects of the projectivity of the point and the instantaneity of the transmission. In fact, memory here is more a matter of passage than of grid. Video-graphic and info-graphic projectivity renews the graphic, photo-graphic and cinemato-graphic projection within a continuum, in which uniform and a-dimensional (0-point dimension) movement plays the role of the straight line in geometric space, according to Euclid's postulate.[2] The homography of points aligned in bi- or tri-dimensional space is succeeded by the projectivity of points aligned in quadri-dimensional space-time. These form an instantaneous *defilade* in which matter is replaced by retinal retention: "This is known as the *sensitization time* of a line. This sensitization time is equal to the nth degree of the *composition time* of the image formed by n lines, which is imposed by the physiology of the ocular system. The eye integrates all of the luminous sensations that come in *in less than* twenty milliseconds and merges the images that occur more rapidly, at a frequency of at least 50 per second. We thus have only 20 milliseconds divided by n to compose each line, and that is sometimes not enough. Given an image composed point by point and line by line, if the composition time is more than 20 milliseconds, the first lines begin to vanish before the last ones appear. . . This inconvenience came be remedied if the screen has a memory so that a line remains visible for a period longer than the composition time."[3]

Thus speed becomes the sole vector for electronic representation, not only inside the micro-processor but in the terminal screen-writing itself: the numeric image.

The crisis of the notion of dimension then appears as a crisis of the whole, a crisis of substantive, continuous and homogeneous space inherited from classical geometry, in favor of the relativity of an accidental, discontinuous and heterogeneous space, one in which the parts and the fractions, the points and the various fragments become once more essential, as if they were an instant, a fraction or fragmenting of time. Which would, as already noted, assail the image of the world as a City, the view of objects in an environment in which inertia has become manifest: "Duration consists of instants without perceptible duration, just as the line is made of points without sensible dimension."[4]

We now can understand the recuperated significance of transparence. At present, transparence replaces appearance because the aesthetics of accelerated disappearance has displaced that of the progressive emergence of forms and figures in their material support, their surface of inscription, from the surfaces of engraving, drawing, painting, sculpture, and the photogravure of intaglio negatives to the monoliths and constructions of architecture. Where once the aesthetics of the appearance of an analogical, stable image of static nature predominated, we now have the aesthetics of the disappearance of a numerical, unstable image of fleeting nature, whose persistence is exclusively retinal — namely, that of the sensitization time, which eludes our conscious attention, once the threshold of 20 milliseconds was crossed — just as with the invention of the ultra-speed camera, whose one million images per second exceeded the composition time of 24 images per second.

☿   ☿   ☿

"Precision is the relationship of measured value to the value of its uncertainty. One could say that precision is its inverse: relative uncertainty."[5] Against aesthetics (coming from *esthesis,* meaning 'unmeasured'), metrology, or "the science of measurement," allows us to observe the history of referents and successive standards that, in the evolution of science, have allowed increasingly precise evaluations of distances, lengths as well as durations of time. Thus we have length and distance of a space of time, of a continuum which has continuously undergone the metamorphoses of engines and the successive and metamorphic deformations of machines of displacement and communication. Meanwhile, these machines have contributed — under the guise of measurement instruments — to the constant redefinition of perceived and of lived space, and thus indirectly to the increasingly rigorous determination of the image of the sensible world: the world of geometry, geography, geomorphology of constructed spaces, and so forth. These are measurement instruments of relative uncertainty and not, as we like to pretend, of a certain inexactitude. These instruments are parallel to and are as necessary as those of the so-called exact sciences. Both contribute to the cultural interpretation of extension as of duration, in a natural environment under perpetual scientific and aesthetic reconstruction. This reconstruction is based on the intelligibility of elements, and also on the more-or-less grand sensibility of vectors of displacement — especially those of communication and telecommunication, that simultaneously displace people and objects as well as the image and representations of the sensible world.

Let us consider the history of this science of measurement, from the eighteenth century, beginning first between 1735 and 1751, the years of the "Voyage around the Equator to Measure one Degree of terrestrial Meridian" by La Condamine and his companions. They performed an epic pilgrimage, intended to discover the most exact form-image of the globe, rather than, as previously, new lands to colonize. From there, we move to the official birth of metrology in 1789 — when the Constitutional Assembly decided to define a unit of national length, with the measurement of the Dunkirk / Barcelona meridianal arc by Delambre and Mechain — and, between 1792 and 1799, the revolutionary invention of the official meter, one ten-millionth part of one-fourth of the terrestrial meridian, which would supplant the units of measure of the Ancien Régime, units which referred to the physiological body and often to the body of the King himself.

We find the same problems in the two geodesic experiments: in the first, problems penetrating the milieu, and in the second, problems transmitting given data. In 1735, for example, the measuring expeditions for the Quito Meridian encountered a particularly hostile environment, struggling in a land with only the roads left by the Incas, since the first communications route between Manta and Quito would only be built in 1739. The measurers, as they travelled on foot and crossed perilously free-swinging footbridges, were hunted by wild animals and local natives alike.

In the second instance, in 1792, the triangulation involving Dunkirk and Barcelona occurred in a revolutionary climate, with all the difficulties of communication and information that marked the landscapes of the day. Unlike La Condamine and Bouguer, Delambre and Mechain set the base of their first triangulation along the rectilinear road that joins Melun to Lieusaint.

In both cases, however, cities served as references points for measuring: Manta and Quito in Latin America, Dunkirk and Barcelona in Europe. Thus we must recognize that along with the actual instruments of scientific measurement, such as the perch, the fathom-measure, the surveyor's transit, contemporary vehicles played an important role. There were dynamic vehicles — such as the horse, the mule, the dugout canoe, the boat — and there were static vehicles — such as the footpath, the road, the rectilinear route, the bridge. Finally, there was the need to level the landscape for surveying, the consequent use of Indian laborers in the more rugged plains, and the importance of the rectilinear character of the route used as baseline by Delambre and Mechain.

All of this should illustrate the already obvious complementarity — forced and always hidden — of the properly scientific instrument of measure and the technical means of communication. The machinery that displaces people and transmits facts and messages is a vehicular complex, formed essentially of a *stationary* vehicle that permits penetration as the relatively easy displacement of the highway, bridge, or tunnel, for example, and a *dynamic* vehicle that authorizes generally longer voyages of boats and various mounts. Without these two, neither the "filming" nor any direct measure could have occurred, certainly not at the scale of the geodesic ambitions of these planetary surveyors.

From this emerged the subsequent need to conserve the "standard meter" and the careful production of that famous platinum ruler deposited in the National Archives in 1799. This primary standard prefigured the iridized platinum version that was deposited at the Breteuil Pavillion in 1875. In the 1875 standard, the distance between its polished, level and parallel extremities represented 1/40 millionth of a terrestrial meridian. That distance also represented a kind of reduced model of the most extreme precision of the standard route from Melun to Lieusaint.

If the history of measurement and the figuring of physical quantities plays a central role in the evolution of scientific knowledge and theory, then one must take into account the increased dematerialization of the referents. The history begins with physical bodies, geodesic measurements, and primary standards using precious metals. But then — with the appearance of Fizeau's interferometer, and the development of Rowland's spectroscopy — the standard is based less on materials than on light and luminous interferences, until, with the Michaelson–Morley experiments with the constancy of the speed of light, the length of a wave of atomic radiation becomes the basis for defining a unit of length.

This displacement of direct ocular observation in favor of optic equipment gave way to the indirect perception of the new instruments of measurement. This story is paralleled by the seemingly natural shift from "primary standards" to transfer standards, from the measured and surveyed material to the measuring light. All of these inaugurate a mutation in the scientific evaluation of time and of space, one which today introduces the crisis — as well as the abandonment — of the dissection of physical dimensions, and hence the pressing necessity for a readjustment of the form-image of the sensible world.

For example, the 1799 rectification of surfaces and superficies (through the leveling of the earth for surveying purposes, the rectilinear route, the pure and hard materials used for standard measures of level, polished, parallel surfaces) gave way, in 1879, with the Michelson experiment's utilization of an experimental vacuum, to the development of a primary vacuum in a steel tube almost two kilometers long and .60 meter in diameter. Measuring the perspective depth no longer demands laying down a road and cutting through forests. Now, all you need to do is create a vacuum in a rectilinear tube so as to allow one ray of light to pass through. No more roads to be laid, no more surfaces to be levelled. Now one produces vacuum out of volume. Now we can work without having to deal with the vicissitudes of the terrain and the lushness of the vegetation. We can even ignore the atmosphere, the very air we breathe.

You know the rest, the radar fall-out after the Second World War, the use of radio-electric high frequencies at varying levels, until the development of the stable laser. In 1960, at the time of the Eleventh General Conference of Weights and Measures, held in Paris, a unit of length was defined as follows: "The meter is the length equal to 1,650,763.73 lengths of a wave in the vacuum of radiation corresponding to the transition between the 2p10 and the 5d5 levels of the Krypton 86 atom." Seven years later, the Thirteenth General Conference adopted an analogous definition for the unit of time: "The second is the duration of 9,192,631,770 periods of radiation corresponding to the transition between the two hyperfine levels of the Cesium 133 atom in its fundamental state."

These perfectly abstract definitions became material in practice through the new standards, the famous "transfer standards": the Krypton lamp for the meter, the Cesium atomic clock for the second. The unit of time, the second, remained the most precise basic unit in the international system of measures, but with the recent development of the stable laser (thanks to the most advanced military research), the precision of the unit of length proved inadequate. Thus, after the last evaluation of the speed of light in 1972, a definition was proposed in which the meter would be merely "the length crossed by light in a vacuum in 1/299,792,458 of a second."[7]

Separated from the measurement of the earth and increasingly precise appreciation of matter, moving from the precious metal standard to that of atoms and molecules, we now enter into the supremacy of light, into a measurement that demands more and more of its speed of diffusion so as to project the form-image of a natural environment, one in which spatial length and temporal distances are merged and confused into a purely numerical representation, a synthetic image that does not come from direct observation nor from the order of optic visualization devised by Galileo. This image comes from electromagnetic receivers, from spectral analyzers and from "frequency meters" in which the acquisition of data is arranged by the computer.

How are we to assess an ostensibly experimental science that always opts for the most extreme vacuum, the highest speeds, and the increasing mediatization of its own means of investigation and communication? How can we no longer believe our own eyes and then believe so easily in the vectors of electronic representation, or in the vector-speed of light? Are we in the presence of an obscurantism of relativity? Is this some new solar cult?

THE LOST DIMENSION

This is not about the disruptive influence of some means of communication. This concerns the instruments of measurement, the standard of transfer, and the machine-transfer, which have no common link to our faculties of appreciation and to our perception of reality. The technical apparatus has become the scientific proof. Numerical information systems produce the exact digit, and the computer screen shows the image, but it is a synthetic, opto-electronic image whose only "dimension" is that of the vector of execution or that of the emission of the light of speed. It comes from a "false day" that has no tie whatsoever to the day of ocular or optic experimental observation.

Flaubert proclaimed, "The more developed the telescope, the more stars there will be." In fact, if the apparatus is the irrefutable proof, then the most technologically advanced equipment is the advancement of the sciences! Basically, if the sciences once were at the origin of technological development, we are now witnessing a reversal, in which the advancement of cutting-edge technologies, spurred by military research, provoke the development of sciences — or, better, of one, new, parcelled and atomized science, in which scientific thought is increasingly conditioned by statistics, by the hidden deliria of automation applied to scientific investigation and production. And this occurred long before robotics took over industrial and post-industrial production.

In the face of this remarkable eviction of direct observation, in the face of this automatic diagnostics, this increased mediatization of all scientific knowledge, this elimination of immediate consciousness and then of the person of the seeker and the worker, we could even ask ourselves if this post-science is not some insidious form of warfare, a pure, intellectual and conceptual warfare that is less attached to the destruction than to the *de-realization* of the world, a de-realization in which scientific–industrial logic supplants political–military strategy, just as that strategy, many centuries ago, supplanted the tactic of the hunter.

The space-time of the opto-electronic representation of the world no longer involves the physical dimensions of geometry. Depth no longer involves the visual horizon, nor the vanishing point of perspective. Depth now pertains exclusively to the primitive grandeur of speed, the grandeur of this new void, the vacuum of speed, that replaces all extension and all depth of field, including geometry and geophysics. The dimension of depth now installs the solar star, the ray of light, as a supreme referent, as a standard of measure for the earth: beyond meridians; beyond fathoms; beyond meters; beyond matter and atoms — since, as we know, it was the 21 centimeter ray of the hydrogen molecule that was carried into sidereal space by the Pioneer satellite to figure the dimensions of our own solar system.

The center of the universe is no longer the geocentric earth or the anthropocentric human. It is now the luminous point of a helio-centrism, or, better yet, of a lumino-centrism, one that special relativity helped install, whose uncontrolled ambitions derive from the purposes of general relativity.

Thus, in the new representations of the form-image of the sensible world, the "point of light" replaced the vanishing point of perspectivists. The luminous point became the vanishing point of the speed of light, the non-place of its acceleration, a photon, electron acceleration that contributes to the present formation of the dimensions of infinite space, just as the point without dimension of ancient Greek geometry served to establish the dimensions of the finite world, including the development of arithmetic and mathematic numeration, as well as the geometric and geographic formulation of the image-form of the "planetary globe."

⊛　⊛　⊛

Another index of this return swing by the pendulum of scientific thinking occurs in the present debate on the beginnings of the universe. The majority of astrophysicists favor the standard model — the Big Bang — against those who hold to the stationary model of an isotropic, homogeneous universe, one having a history identical in each point. For the partisans of the standard model of an expanding universe, the scientific interest centers on the point of departure, the creation of the world, the origin of space, time and matter.

In these two cosmological conceptions, the question of the physical depth of space redoubles the duality of the historical depth of time. According to Evry Schatzman, "If we take into account the fact that the observation is made by means of light, and that that moves at a finite speed, then the objects are observed in a past that is itself as distant as they are remote."[8] Speaking later of the theory of the beginning of the universe, he continues, "Operating on such large distances and extremely large time intervals, at the boundaries of the possibilities of experimentation, allows us to imagine a new physics, modifying the constant basics, rejecting their character as constants in order to create expanses dependent on time." In other words, expanses that depend exclusively on speed, the primitive expanse of the constant of the speed of light, a constant that will permit us to reform all of the basic constants of physics. No more and no less than that.

Isn't this a new sort of illuminism? Isn't this really a latter-day solar cult hiding under the grandest of scientific pretensions around, that of knowing the origin of origins, including the origins of light, matter, space and time? Isn't this especially the case if — as a number of physicists have noted — "climbing sufficiently far back into the past, the idea of origin ends up by losing its meaning."[9]

Is this a point of departure or a point of suspension? To answer this, let us return to Schatzman, whose theory of the expanding universe is likewise a theory of its infinite contraction: "This rests on the physical fact of a homogeneous, isotropic universe in which all the parts are attracted to each other according to Newton's Law, and necessarily find themselves either in a state of expansion or contraction. Finite or infinite, the universe and every fraction thereof is condemned to struggle against attraction by movement." This dromological vision of the universe promotes the exclusive importance of the Newtonian cosmology, the central role of the constant of gravity, as well as the centrality of the constant of the speed of light, the two essential constants — along with that of Max Planck — of current physics. According to Schatzman, "The existence of gravity allows a difficult escape from expansion. For every value of density in the universe there exists a minimum speed of expansion if it is to avoid collapsing in on itself. It is for this that the kinetic energy of movement compensates exactly the potential energy due to gravity."[10]

Strangely enough, the Newtonian cosmology involves the necessity of an explosive universe, or — after an initially dense state of contraction, and practically unlimited inertial confinement — space-time would have exploded in a spectacular, blinding light preceding all particles of matter. All of this explains the "gravitational catastrophe" as the unique motor force of the cosmos.

Should we now be surprised at this sublimation of explosion? The creation of the world, the mode of production of all substance and matter, found its origin in accidence, the mode of destruction of a deflagration, for which the high pressures of the cannon's combustion chamber provided a model. Physics and astrophysics found their common theoretical basis in the war machine. The machinery of pure war was conceived in the progress of the advanced experimental sciences that emerged from the arsenal, even more directly than from Galileo's experiments in Venice.

In the catastrophic model, gunpowder, the artillery tube, the bullet and ballistics of the first master-artillerymen of the eighteenth century became archetypes. The cannon of the exact sciences appeared first in the cinematic perception of the parabolic movement of the planets, and then in the understanding of their principles of motion, the energetic consciousness of a force that acts between planets: gravitation. It would be futile to deny the links between the progress made in ballistics and that of the astronomical sciences, from Galileo to Descartes. Descartes' analytical geometry, and its coordinates, underwrites more than our appreciation of the point as a basis for the organization of motion, extension, and grid memory. In 1634 Descartes wrote to his friend Paul Mersenne, "if a cannonball could escape weight." In response, Mersenne, who would measure the speed of sound two years later, thought of pointing a cannon straight up, hoping that the projectile could stay up forever. In this, he designed an experiment that was analogical to and exactly the inverse of Galileo's.

Leonard Euler, the renowned mathematician and astronomer, also devised the curved shooting method still used by artillery soldiers today. Let us not forget that Jean Victor Poncelet was a general in the French Army in 1812, when he invented projective geometry. Remember Hemoltz's experiments in the arsenal at Munich.

Finally, what do we make of the philosophers' histories of reference? Since Antiquity, philosophers and scientists referred to the movement of projectiles of the first generation, such as the arrow and the cannonball. Then, with Einstein, Louis de Brolie, Heisenberg, they all switched to the vehicles of the second generation, such as the train, the plane, firing shell, the rocket. Then they moved with Bergson, Walter Benjamin, Deleuze and Barthes towards the different vectors of technical representation, such as photography, cinematography, holography. All this ends up with Stephen

Weinberg and Ilya Prigogine, Nobel-Prized physicists, redis-covering Plato's cave, the magic box of the pre-rational origins of science.

These days it is almost required that one affirm the magical and symbolic aspect of the sphere, of the circle, of the center and its periphery. From the high epochs of cosmogony right down to Einstein in 1916 — explaining gravitation as the result of a spatio-temporal curvature of the universe — we rigorously exclude the influence of the cylinder and of the tubular form in our modern intellectual histories, beginning with hydraulics, the innovation of eyeglasses and of the stethoscope, which was the first audio-visual media. This history then passes from Huyghens' 1673 invention of the mono-cylindrical motor (in which the cannon is described as the "first internal combustion engine ever," the first automo-bile media), down through the already mentioned "vacuum tube," and then to Michelson's experiments and on to the electron cannon, to the cathode tube, to contemporary laser technology with the present use of the optic cavity of the coherent ray of light, or the optic-fiber cable, allowing centers of telecommunication to advance from analogic commutation to temporal commutation.

Tubular forms have played an important role in recent developments in science and technology. For example, in topology we find Euler, once more, resolving a famous problem of urban warfare, that of the seven points of the City of Konigsburg. The solution to this strategic problem of rates and directions of city traffic later produces systems theory, which then benefits economics and communications and telecommunications networks.

Basically, if the early sciences were sciences of the earth, of matter and of physical sciences, sciences of sub-stance such as geology and physiology, then the contempo-rary or post-modern late sciences appear as sciences of accidence: accidents of energy, accidents of electrological and luminological transfer that have to do with fluids and different kinds of radiance and radiation.

From matter to light, scientific knowledge progressively avoids any reference to solids or solid references points, as they submit increasingly to the impact of advanced technologies and, thus, give up on their required material proofs. For contemporary physics, this poses the major and thus far unnoticed technological danger, of a kind of delirium of interpretation due to the excess of mediation of experiences, in which the rapport, the relation of the subject to the object of the experiment, could be definitively lost, to the dubious credit of form-images of the rapidly shortening scientific course. We are facing a cinematism of scientific representation, detached from all human, ethical, and soon even scientific, constraint or context. Where we once had art for the sake of the art of theoretical conception, now we have science for the science of a magico-statistical representation of the world, of which the recent enumeration of the elementary particles offers an example of the trend.

Are we prepared to accept a reversal of all philosophic meaning, hereafter considering accident as absolute and necessary, and substance — all substance — as relative and contingent, hereafter considering catastrophe not as substantial deformation but rather as an unexpected accidental formation *à la* René Thom, and, further, to consider movement and acceleration not as displacement but rather as emplacement, an emplacement without any precise place, without geometric or geographic localization, as with the particles of quantum mechanics? We must at least resolve ourselves to losing the sense of our senses, common sense and certainties, in the material of representation. We must be ready to lose our morphological illusions about physical dimensions; except for the point, the *punctum,* that figurative abstraction more resistant than the atom and, as always, absolutely necessary for different conceptions of the world.

Here we arrive at the third constant of modern physics, Max Planck's constant, affirming in 1900 that radiating energy, like matter, has a discontinuous structure, and can only exist in the form of a grain (a quanta of HV value, in which H is a universal constant of 6,624 x 10-27 CGS, and V is the frequency of emission, or radiation). Punctum, quantum; with Heisenberg's uncertainty principle and Planck's constant, not only was the difference between matter and light blurred, but also the notions of space and time became invalidated.

The crisis of the physical dimensions of the sensible world in the era of electronic telecommunications derives from the crisis of the intelligible continuum. We approach grains of matter or of light without distinction, since they are not localizable in the space-time framework. As Louis de Broglie explains, we are participating in a radical inversion: "Neither time nor space, statistical concepts, allow us to describe the properties of elementary entities, of grains. To the contrary, from statistical methods developed from the manifestations of elementary entities, a sufficiently competent theory could elicit the framework of our macroscopic perceptions that form time and space." Pursuing this description, de Broglie continues: "We can see the continuous frame constituted by our space-time as engendered in a kind of Heisenberg's uncertainty, the macroscopic continuity resulting thus from a statistics operated on the discontinuous elements that are affected by uncertainty."[12]

Thus, space and time would be no more than macroscopic statistical realities, and the grain, the quantum, would be "that indivisible physical entity, that discontinuous element that in the depths of the infinitely small appears to constitute ultimate reality. . ."

In order to fully articulate the scientific performance of the uncertainty relationship, de Broglie unflinchingly exceeds the boundaries of theoretical research in declaring:

"Real quantum physics will undoubtedly be a physics that, renouncing all ideas of positions, instants, objects and all that which constitutes our common sense, will bid farewell to purely quantum notions and hypotheses and, elevating itself to the level of macroscopic statistical phenomena, will show us how quantum reality at the atomic level can emerge, by the play of means, the frame of space time valid for the human dimension."

The new science's rattling of the spatio-temporal framework used by classical physics also involves a crisis of determinism. In ancient mathematical physics, the space-time grid was a given. Into this framework came the physical entities, and their evolution was considered as rigorously determined, deriving from an initial state that was supposedly known by differential equations or by partial derivatives. Such was the view of pre-quantum physics: it realized in large strokes the description of figures and movements that Descartes longed for.

But quantum physics sees something else altogether. Relations of uncertainty stand against that which we can never know at the same moment, the figure and the movement. In the case of an elementary particle, we either measure its speed and ignore its position, or else we know its exact position as we ignore its speed. In 1982, Alain Aspect, physician of the Optic Institute at Orsay, confirmed as much in an experiment of historical consequences.[13]

① ① ①

Some might see this long detour through physics as needlessly, even uselessly, arduous, but that would be to ignore and misread the effects of models, the effect of the reality of theoretical models on practical geometry, the space and time of different spatial, architectonic and urbanistic representations. The crisis of physical dimensions, just as the crisis of measurement, is tied up with the crisis of determinism[14] and affects today the whole ensemble of representations of the world.

Once we know the importance of figures, of movement and of extension in the organization and direction of space, we can easily predict the effects of their statistical relativization and sudden de-realization at the "hands" of the technologies of computer-assisted representation. If the *theoretical* representation at the *microscopic* level of atomic particles is now the fact of quantum mechanics, which is the quantum of action and energy, this neutron, electron or photon grain of matter or of light, and the uncertainty of its speed and its position in a fundamentally uncertain environment, then at the *macroscopic* level of humans, the *practical* representation is now the effect of a sort of alpha-numerical punctum mechanics which — while seemingly sacrificing the grid of Cartesian coordinates — nevertheless and essentially relies on the video-performances of a punctum of action, the pixel or luminous point of electronic optics, the synthetic form-image resulting not only from properties of the programmer's program but also and above all from the vector-speed of its effectuation, the vector-speed of the elementary particles (electrons) that reminds us that "telematics" is not only the fact of binding informatics with instantaneous transmission across great distances. Telematics is first of all the instantaneity effect of the immediate broadcasting of a figure, its movement or its apparent extension through the interface of a screen. This analogical or numerical figure comes from the very absence of a field, of a depth of field, so that depth is now only that which occurs in the temporal video-performances of the pixel.

The classical opposition between notions of continuous field and discontinuous grain or point finds itself once more in the ambiguity of the notion of interface, or, better, in the present mutation of the ancient limitation into commutation — commutation which has ceased to be analogical (as in continuous physical value, length, angles) in order to become numerical (as numbers or discontinuous enumeration) or temporal. We can now see more clearly the theoretical and practical importance of the notion of interface, that drastically new surface that annuls the classical separation of position, of instant or object, as well as the traditional partitioning of space into physical dimensions, in favor of an almost instantaneous configuration in which the observer and the observed are roughly linked, confused, and chained by an encoded language from which emerges the ambiguity of interpretation of represented form-images, an ambiguity that returns to that of audio-visual media, especially that of live television and of the uncertainty of the televised images, as well as the geometry of their re-transmission (and this despite the use of systems theories).

The ambiguity of interpretation at stake here has nothing to do with the order of intellegibility of its factors, such as memorized data or numerical and digital figures. It concerns the more-or-less grand sensibility of "vectors," vectors of representation which, in the electronic interface, affect the order of sensations, and, above all, the capacity to have or to not have sensations. From this comes the growing, creeping, neutralization, on television for example, of broadcast journalists and tele-spectators who wait for the "first material light" of mediated information. Indeterminacy affects not only the domains of particle physics and of the philosophy of action. It also disturbs, despite all appearances to the contrary, those of statistics and information systems.[16]

The imbalance between the direct information of our senses and the mediated information of the advanced technologies is so great that we have ended up transferring our value judgments and our measure of things from the object to its figure, from the form to its image, from reading episodes of our history to noting their statistical tendencies. As part of

52

this grand transferal, we now face the major technological danger of a generalized delirium of interpretation.

For example, when we write that instantaneous transparence has replaced successive appearances of things and figures, that does not mean that we are recuperating some space of time, some morphological continuum. No. Instead we encounter in the interface a form-image in which time more than space makes the "surface," since the only depth is that of the primitive dimension of speed, the emptiness of the quick, that of the vector of instantaneous transmission of data that affects, with the consciousness of the users, the figures, the movements and the represented extension.

To better understand the rediscovered importance of this notion of transparence, connected to that of interface, the advent of this future world beyond this one of sensible appearances, we return to the work of Benoit Mandelbrot, and especially his notion of dimension: "What exactly is a physical dimension? It is an intuitive notion that seems to have originated with ancient Greek geometry. It deals with relations between figure and objects, the first term necessarily concerning mathematical idealizations, while the latter deals with real data and facts. From this perspective, objects, even the tiniest ball or the sheerest veil or the finest thread, must be represented by three dimensional figures, in the exact same manner as a large, coarse ball. But, in fact, every physicist knows that we must proceed differently, and that it is more useful to think that the veil, the thread, or the ball, if they are sufficiently fine, are respectively closer to the second, first and zero dimensions — (we note here the practical usefulness of the account of the large, of the gross as of the small, stories connected to the anthropomorphic characteristics of the observer). — In other words, the physical dimension inevitably has a pragmatic, and hence subjective, base; *it concerns the degree of resolution.* As confirmation, remember that a complex object, such as a ball of thread 10 cm in diameter and made up of thread that is 1 mm in diameter, possesses in a somewhat latent manner many distinct physical dimensions. At the 10-meter degree of resolution, it appears as a point, thus as a zero-dimensional figure. At the 10-centimeter degree of resolution, it is a ball, and thus a three-dimensional figure. At the 10-millimeter degree of resolution, it is a construction of threads, and thus a one-dimensional figure. At the 0.1-mm degree of resolution, each thread becomes a kind of column, and the whole becomes again a three-dimensional figure. At the 0.01-mm degree of resolution, each column dissolves into filiform fibers and the whole is once again a uni-dimensional figure, and thus we see the determination of the dimension continuously jumping around. At a certain level of analysis, the ball of thread is represented as a finite number of infinitesimally small atoms, and the whole once more is zero-dimensional."[17]

As this approach illuminates the analogical observation and the numerical resolution of represented figures, it also illustrates the transparence and the technical means of transparence accrued from the appearances of the represented object: advancing towards the ball from 10 meters to 10 cm, then followed by the use of additional magnifying lenses, then of microscopes of higher and higher magnification or video-magnification. This displacement is not neutral; as with all movement, each displacement (human, ocular, optic, opto-electronic) engages a specific speed, and this speed affects the representation under consideration and provokes a kind of rupture or severance which, while it may not be dimensional in the strict, archaic sense of the word, certainly has an impact on the resultant scientific observation. From this emerges the notorious oscillation of the dimensional value, a cinematic jumping that would not exist if we took account of the "speed vector" of both the defilading and the observation that go into enchaining into one long sequence-plan the different scales of vision and the diverse degrees of resolution of the image, thereby attaining an unparalleled transparence.

It is precisely the magnitude of speed, a hitherto unequalled magnitude, a "depth of time," that eludes the habitual limitations that result from the material resistance, just as with the more-or-less distant localizations of observed objects. The severance of dimensions — whether considered as entities from 0 to 3, or as fractions as Mandelbrot prefers — is thus not strictly a facet of the observed object, having to do with degrees of resolution of figures and of images. It is also the effect of different filming sequences, and of the more-or-less high rapidity of execution of their montage: cinematic, cinematographic, or videographic montage, of which the constant progress of the means of communication of dimension (such as the telescope, microscope, or telemeasure) has finally made us aware, optic or opto-electronic means that are no different than those of televisual or telematic telecommunications; or, again, those means of physical transport of people, since it always comes back to that primitive magnitude of the rapid vehicle, such as the TGV or the Concorde, that turns Paris into a neighborhood of Valence and makes New York the great suburb of the Ile de France.

If, as suggested by relativity theory, speed expands time in the instant it contracts space, we arrive finally at the negation of the notion of physical dimension, and we must ask once more, "What is a dimension?" Mandelbrot repeats that this is a matter of the degree of resolution, and that the numerical result depends on the relations between the object and the observer. That is, it depends on the nature of the difference between the observed and the one observing, the physical dimension acting merely as fragmentary messages that ancient geometry endlessly interpreted — or, better, misinterpreted — and from which came the optical illusion of entire, or unitary, dimensions, an illusion which arose from the inadequacy of ancient methods of observation.

This is exact, but incomplete, since the true "dimension," *dimensus* as measure, involves not only the degree of resolution of the geometric and mathematic form-image under consideration, but also its celerity, the value of its dimensional mediation, continuously transforming itself, through dromoscopic oscillation, at the pleasure of the progress of the speed of configuration, the means of communication of dimension, such as surveyor, lens, and telemeasure, being simultaneously the means of extermination of the approximated dimension.

This is what we find in Richardson's measurements of the approximate length of the coast of Brittany, which turns out to be an *inverse measure* of the arc of the earth's meridian as worked out in the eighteenth century by La Condamine and his fellow surveyors. But this time the rectification of the route and the levelling of the earth, far from being sought after, were instantly rejected. "If the coast had been straight, the problem would have been resolved," explains Mandelbrot, "but since this wild coast is extremely sinuous, one can imagine a man who walks the length of the coast by committing himself to turning as little as possible. In this way, that man measures the distance he has covered. Then we do it over by making the maximal distance of this person on the shoreline smaller and smaller. At a given moment, in the service of exactitude, we replace the man with a mouse, the mouse with a fly, and so on. The closer we get to the actual coast, the greater the distance to be covered. This is inevitable. *The final distance will be so great that we can practically consider it infinite...* One way or another, anthropocentrism intervenes," according to Mandelbrot, "and the seemingly inoffensive concept of geographic distance is not entirely objective, since the observer inevitably intervenes in its definition."[18]

Measurement is thus displacement. One not only displaces oneself, in order to take the measure, but one also displaces the territory in its representation, in its geometric or cartographic reduction. We force its morphological reality into a geodesic configuration, one possessing a merely relative and momentary value.

Giving dimensions is like phase-displacement in electronics. Here the displaced phase is that of the observer, the geometer, the visionary–surveyor producing the measure in the instant in which he provokes its displacement. But this movement that produces size and approximate length can be accelerated by the use of technologies of displacement, such as transport or transmission. This is what is missing in the study of variations of approximate length of the coast of Brittany, and it is this that is hidden in the seemingly inoffensive declaration, "If the coast were straight, the problem would be resolved." Rigorously absent is the temporal aspect of all acts of measurement and of all acts of sighting, an aspect that has become increasingly evident with recent developments among the advanced technologies of transportation and transmission, as well as telemeasurement. The figures of the man, the mouse, and the fly who survey the Breton coastline are only the anthropomorphic and zoomorphic aspects of a specific speed of displacement. If we imagine for a moment a faster vector of displacement for each of these subjects, everything is once again metamorphosed. On the one hand, the distance tends towards infinity; this is the morphological aspect of the problem. On the other, and simultaneous, hand, the approximate distance approaches zero, by dint of the acceleration of the actual act of measuring. This happens irrespective of the nature of the surveyor, since that "nature" is inseparable from its speed of displacement. Thus, the notorious straight line acts as the resolution of the problem of the measure of the length of the coast of Britanny, and the resolution of its form-image, re-inscribing itself for the surveyor into this "depth of time," this duration or length of time in which speed has become the privileged vector.

We now have two kinds of accidents, two kinds of

sinuosities slicing the measured coastline. We have terrain accidents due to macro- and microscopic reliefs, and we have the transfer accidents of physical transport and electronic transmission, due to changes in the speed of the surveyor, this "reading head" of the continuum.

Here another question occurs. If the straight line is the shortest distance between two points, should we read Euclid's postulate as a sublimation of speed? In effect, since the turn of the century, we have witnessed the progressive disappearance of distance-space, in meters and kilometers, and, more recently, with the development of high-speed technologies, such as telemetrics, telematics, and supersonics, the allegedly ideologically progressive disappearance of distance-time. The measure of extension and of movement is now almost exclusively that of a technical vector, a mode of communication or telecommunication that desynchronizes the time from the space of the passage. This happened when geometry went through its own phase-displacement in its attempt to develop dimensions, submitting terrains and the entire earth to the displacement systems of geometric and geodesic representation. Today, we must begin to recognize that the systems and instruments of measurement are less chronometric than cinemetric. The standard for measuring the space traveled through is no longer the time of passage but rather the speed, the distance-speed, which has become the measure and the privileged dimension of space as of time.

In supersonic transports, for example, the speedometer no longer records the kilometers. Instead, the machometer measures nothing more than the intensity of acceleration, that is, the relationship of the speed of an object to the speed of sound in the atmosphere it is displacing. But this "basic unit of measure" is not a true unit of speed, for the speed of sound is itself proportional to the square root of the absolute temperature. The final unit of measure, the final standard of transfer, is once more the absolute speed, the speed of light. We enter yet again into the latter-day solar cult, in which the rays of sunlight have become the standard of relativity and the standard of transfer for all reality.

The light of speed illuminates the world and all its matter in the very instant in which it offers up its representation. But this is a representation for which the violence of its fusion and the power of its emission have replaced the course of the sun from dawn to dusk.

Basically, day and night stopped organizing the life of the city in that instant in which space and time lost their practical importance in favor of an accrued transparence that is also an accrued depth. This is a cinemetric depth, in which light suddenly acquired the cosmological status of primary substance. In this false day, there is no longer any palpable difference between the hidden space of microscopic representations and the visible space of macroscopic perceptions. Out of this morphological irruption emerges that confusion, carefully maintained, between space and its form-image and between time and its technical de-realization. An identical synoptic unveiling is at work here: great distances no longer hide the appearances of distant lands, the opacity of materials no longer hides the intimate details of matter. This "transparence" — not to be confused with any physical dimension, as a non-separability that is both quantic, or infinitely small, and optic, actually opto-electronic, or infinitely large — should lead us back, after Euclid, whose postulate allows for speed, to Galileo, whose small telescope, whose astronomer's lens, prefigured the highest speeds of motion. This resulted in the previously mentioned ambiguity of interpretation, the conflict between Catholic theology and scientific teleology, which is the subject of form-images in the new optics, for which the scientist was destroyed.

Finally, this interpretative conflict between astronomy and the Church about the form and movement of the planet was meant to conceal an essential aspect in which glimmered for the first time, beyond immediate appearances, the primacy of the speed of light, the driving force behind the additional lenses of the first rapid-vector telescope in history, and this, long before propulsion engines, machines that much later would verify the natural vastness of the approximate or tele-observed proximity.[19]

Seventeenth-century theologians were forced to ask a highly pointed question: *"Is a Mass seen by means of a telescope valid? . . . Do we consider the worshipper who tele-observes the dominical liturgy as having actually participated in the religious service?"* Their response was negative, and today participation in televised mass is still reserved for the old, the infirm and the disabled. A number of socio-cultural and geopolitical problems are hidden behind this sort of interpretation, problems that one must be careful not to resolve too hastily, to the extent that they concern urban proximity, the basic unit of physical neighborhoods of the City. Today, the first massive proximity in the history of populating space and managing territories has entered into open conflict with the regime of telecommunication.

At the furthest reaches of teleology and topology, or networks and fluxes, there now exists — though in a latent and yet real manner — a tele-topology of form-images, which is nothing more than the superficial and momentary expression of a twisting, a distortion or warping of vector-velocity, be it of transport or transmission.

The end of the demarcation of surfaces and volumes, as of all physical extensions, in favor of the instantaneous commutation of the interface, goes hand-in-hand with the uncertainty principle, and the recently renewed affirmation of the non-separability of elementary particles in the events of quantum mechanics. In this tele-topological mode, as the *punctum* regains its primary importance and light suddenly becomes prime matter, transparence becomes a substance, a new material which is not exactly space / time and which is not properly analyzed, or filed, until one has attained a degree of unsuspected purity. This "degree of purity" corresponds to the degree of resolution of the form-image under study — be it infinitely large or small — and from which arises the use and the theoretical and practical necessity for vector analysis: the vector-velocity of representation has become the ultimate "dimension" of our perception.

All of this has been proven chemically, with the recent appearance of new materials with analogical properties, such as plexiglass and transparent resins of plastic materials, as well as with innumerable electronic innovations, such as various video screens, terminals or monitors, cathode tubes or matrix screens, plasma screens and holography, all thanks to the "coherent light" of the laser beam. This trend — constant since the *aufklarung* — continued with recent developments in the means of microscopic investigation, as well as with the research into the ultimate cavities of dense matter (by the video performances of the new electron-sweep microscope that gives, inverse to the electron-transmission microscope, the apparent third dimension of the infinitely small, as well as the possibility of "planes in sequence" from different angles).

We are once more confronted with the crisis of whole dimensions, with the notion of the global density of matter. This seems to extend the earlier problem of approximate length. According to Mandelbrot, "We know that the average density of matter decreases continually as we consider increasingly larger volumes, and our observations give no reason to suppose that this trend changes with much larger distances and much lower densities."

In this tele-topological vision, the "entire" universe acts like a ball of thread. Mandelbrot goes on to say, "In the middle zone, its dimension would be less than three; with three large levels, it would be less than or equal to three. In all cases, on a very small scale, from an astronomical point of view, where we find solids fully demarcated, it would equal one and then three."

The morphological irruption no longer spares either the extension or the thickness of matter in the name of the so-called whole dimensions. But, again, since more-or-less dense mass and more-or-less large distances are functions of speed, according to Einstein, this apparent rupture of the continuum does not result from measured, analyzed space. It is an effect of celerity, understood not as "acceleration" so much as *"illumination"* — less speed than subliminal light, the light of the velocity of light that illuminates the world, in the instant in which it offers up its representation.

Since the visible is now only the effect of the surface interface of the promptness of the luminous emission, and since, furthermore, at the ocular level, that which moves increasingly quickly becomes decreasingly perceptible, we have to admit that that which is given to us as perceived is done so by means of phenomena of acceleration and decelera-tion, in each case linked to the intensity of luminescence. If speed is light, then all light becomes semblance, the shifting appearances of momentary and false transparencies, and the dimensions of space become mere fugitive apparitions. All become figures and objects seen in the instant of a glance, but the glance is both the perceived place and the perceiving eye. The glance is at once site and sight.

Thus, speed sources are also light sources and image sources. They are sources for the image-forms of the earth when considering its dimensions. Promoting the apparition and development of high speeds, the scientific and industrial revolutions also contributed to the development of a large number of formula and *clichés* that all refer to the new rep-resentation of different physical sizes. The transport and communications revolution thus incited the industrializa-tion of the artisanal production of appearances, including those of the geometric, pictorial and architectural variety. The manufacturing of speed, and thus of light and images, suddenly became the cinematic projection of reality, the fabrication of the world *and* of a world of artificial images, a montage of sequences in which the optics of motor illusion re-establishes the illusion of optics.

Through the constant re-establishment of relations between appearance and motion (from Copernicus to Newton, via Galileo and Descartes), Western geometry has proceeded to the regulation of diverse forces of *penetration* — such as motor energy, of diverse forms of *representation* — such as cinematic optics. With the re-emergence of appearances, geometry — taking matter as perspective, and thus as an objective dimension — accelerates its dissipation and infinite fragmentation in time, to the extermination of distances and dimensions.

Speed finally allows us to close the gap between physics and metaphysics.

⊛   ⊛   ⊛

When depth of time replaces depths of sensible space; when the commutation of interface supplants the delimitation of surfaces; when transparence re-establishes appearances; then we begin to wonder whether that which we insist on calling *space* isn't actually *light,* a subliminary, para-optical light of which sunlight is only one phase or reflection. This light occurs in a duration measured in instantaneous time exposure rather than the historical and chronological passage of time. The time of this instant without duration is "exposure time," be it over- or under-exposure. Its photographic and cinematographic technologies already predicted the existence and the time of a continuum stripped of all physical dimensions, in which the quantum of energetic action and the punctum of cinematic observation have suddenly become the last vestiges of a vanished morphological reality. Transferred into the eternal present of a relativity whose topological and teleological thickness and depth belong to this final measuring instrument, this speed of light possesses one direction, which is both its size and dimension and which propagates itself at the same speed in all radial directions that measure the universe.

As Dietrich Bonhoeffer wrote some fifty years ago, "Time is a cycle of light." Paraphrasing Leibnitz by replacing "matter" with "light," we can now add: "space is nothing without light." Thus, this matter-light — the energetic apperception of the contemporary cosmos — replaces the *ether* of earlier physicians and metaphysicians.

As we face this hyperrealist conception of the universe — with its sudden deregulation of physical appearances, in which localization and identification progressively lose all meaning, as do distinctions between base, form, position and disposition in space-time — we begin to wonder about the philosophical status of relativity. In his *Poetics of Space,* Bachelard explained, "Every image has a destiny of growth." Basically, that is what happened when the old writing surfaces, whether graphic, photographic, or cinematographic, became interface. This new conception of "support-surfaces" — that accord volume where there is none visibly, as they inversely and simultaneously remove depth — now seem to be replacing numerous terms that used to designate physical properties of space, such as delimitation and dimension, and by tomorrow might designate space-time itself.

For example, when people suggest that space is only a statistical notion, when they forego sensory perceptions in favor of technological apperceptions that challenge the very boundaries of intelligibility (as do those adepts of quantum mechanics and astrophysics when they discuss the beginnings of the universe), they contribute to the transformation of the *mirror* into a *corridor.* This is the prerequisite passage into that scientific narcissism, beyond all reflection, wherein was invented the "transcendental mathematics" of Lewis Carroll, among others, of that mathematical logistics where the representations of the continuous and the discontinuous communicate.[20]

The super-fluidity and super-conductivity observed in certain dense materials submitted to very low temperatures are macroscopic quantum effects; thus they perfectly predict this tele-topological "non-separability": the coming generalization of the notion of interface and the probable growth of the "form-image" that comes from advanced technologies, such as videographic, infographic and holographic images. Finally, interface appears as the practical fall-out of the theoretical and relativist notion of continuum. Without this last notion, the former would never have seen the light of day, (but this day is the metaphysicians' day). It has nothing to do with our daily activities. Its light is not that of astronomy, and comes from no solar star; it is the light of one theory,[21] of a theory of energy that appeared, in 1905, along with cinematography and aviation, the grand vectors of audiovisual and automotive transformation of sensory appearances.

Thus Albert Einstein and, even more, the transport and transmission revolutions, imposed the idea and the ideography of four-dimensioned space, in which rectilinear and uniform movement assumes the role played by the straight line in three-dimensioned Euclidean space. The speed of Euclid's postulate is no longer hidden. Space and time are amalgamated. This fusion / confusion of hitherto irreconcilable variables opens onto other probabilities, in introducing new variables. Thus, hyper-volumes and hyper-space generalize the habitual notions of content, or volume, and superficie, or surface or extension. These generalizations later lead straight to the idea of interface.

Although Hausdorf, in 1919 — three years after the theory of general relativity — already introduced the notion of a generalized dimension able to assume all the possible values (fractions and irrationals), according to von Koch (1904) and Peano (one of the inventors of mathematical logistics and ideography), only recently did someone—Benoit Mandelbrot, Paul Lévy's student at the Polytechnic — develop the principle of infinite fragmentation of physical dimensions.

This drifting of figures and geometric figuring, this irruption of dimensions and transcendental mathematics, leads us to the promised surrealist peaks of scientific theory, peaks that culminate in Gödel's theorem: the existential proof,[22] a method that mathematically proves the existence of an object without producing that object, and a theory that will end with von Neumann, one of the developers of atomic armaments, whose celebrated game theory will serve as the basis for United States nuclear strategy. Following his involvement in a car crash, it was von Neumann who provided a definition of relativist interface, as he declared: "A curious thing happened. The trees on my right were moving in a row at a steady 60 miles per hour, when one of them stepped out of line."[23] Here he reiterates Einstein's definition of the eternal present: "Events don't happen. They are there, and we encounter them en route."

Here, the tree encountered on the road by von Neumann is considered less an object than a figure, a fraction of a figure, an irruption of an energy and cinematic configuration. It is an optical illusion of motor-function, in which space and time are confused in a sort of permanent present. As an accident of energy transfer, or telescoping between the immobile tree and the car, it illustrates the accident of cinematic transfer embodied by Galileo's telescope. In fact, if we look carefully at the term 'telescoping', we find it is made up of two usages: (1) the noun, 'telescope', examines that which is distant; and, (2) the verb, 'to telescope', crushes inward, or condenses without distinction.

The Morphological Irruption

Hence the optical illusion of the lens — approaching the distant to examine it — meets that of the automobile — condensing without distinction the near and the far, the living and the inanimate. The crossing of appearances is wedded here to some disturbance of perception. When the car's route is seen as an abusive interlocking of the far and the near, the role of the automobile as vehicle consists less in transporting the passenger than in sliding aside physical reality, modifying first all lenses, then all optical instruments, and finally all different planes of visual experience. Having abolished our knowledge of distance and dimension, of cognition and recognition, the role of the means of communications moves from displacing the users to detaching them from their immediate environment.

Hugo once wrote, "Form is the base that rises to the surface." This definition of interface touches directly and intimately on this transmutation of sensory appearances, in which the surface has become a momentary surface-effect, the line has become an instantaneous tracer-effect, and volume has become an accelerated perspective. In other words, we have entered the realm of anamorphosis.

Only the point remains, this absence, this suspension of physical dimensions that, unlike the atom, is never broken down since it is the ultimate reality, the figurative reference for all disintegrations, for all mathematical and morphological irruptions, and likewise for all lasting or momentary interruptions, since matter that is extended in space is also and simultaneously extended in time.

Why do we stand amazed before the assumed properties of the black holes of outer space? Aren't all of our puncta of observation and all of our quanta of action simply black holes of scientific thought? These are the black dots of the line wherein begin and end our rational representations. As Bachelard slyly suggested, "The original sin of reason is that of having an origin." According to the most recent theories of the origin of origins, the principle of causality of the universe will not be a primary substance; it will be an accident: an absolute and necessary accident which rendered all subsequent substance relative and contingent. This original accident is to reason and to the human sciences what original sin was to human nature.

In the face of this inversion that affects and will continue to affect the representation of different states of matter, as well as those of architectonics, we can answer Hegel's old question: "How can we obtain a beginning in philosophy?" How? Exclusively through a striking force, an accident that enthrones reason in the space and place of the grace of God — or, if one prefers, of the grace of created substance.

This is why Dietrich Bonhoeffer proclaimed, "Systematic philosophy is despair in terms of its own beginning, as with all beginning."

And finally, the quarrel between theology and teleology never ended. Ever since Galileo, it was simply displaced from the increasingly precise measurements of space and time onto the immeasurable excesses of an instant without duration and without dimension. An instant in which constructive reason finds its destiny.

3
Improbable Architecture

According to Walter Benjamin, architecture, like cinema, "presents material to a simultaneous collective reception."[1] This is what filmmaker René Clair meant when he claimed, "The art that is closest to cinema is architecture."

This sudden confusion between the reception of images from a film projector and the perception of architectonic forms clearly indicates the importance of the transformation of the notion of "surface" and of "face-to-face" that gives way to the appearance of the interface. In this regard, Benjamin's terms are particularly revealing. Matter, for example, like architecture, is no longer even what it pretends to be, since this matter is "light." It is the light of an emission, of an instantaneous projection that results in a reception rather than a perception. Furthermore, the collective and worldly nature of this "reception" again clearly indicates that the architectural representation no longer acts as one aspect among many. It is now simultaneously all aspects, all points of view and lines of vision, for all the actor–spectators in all constructed space, for the whole population who directly receive the transmission of the architectonic form-image.

We already know that all representation involves reduction of scale, proportion, content, or nature. But now reduction is rejected, for the simultaneous collective response acts as a ubiquitous eye that sees everything at once. Thus it is significant that Benjamin's text opens with a passage from Paul Valery's "The Conquest of Ubiquity." In effect, Benjamin's earlier phrase installs architectural space in an "alter-world," an alter-world that cinematographic techniques, building on photographic antecedents, tried to conquer. These included the multiple superimposed images of Gance and Eisenstein, Painleve's rapid- and slow-motion filming, and the systematic use of new means of transport — such as camera rigs, trains, elevators, airplanes and so forth — by people like Fromiaut, Vertov, Griffith, and Moholy-Nagy. We see that the material presented by architecture to the simultaneous reception is, in fact, the total matter of materialism itself — and especially of historical materialism — that gives its meaning and dimension to time and history, as well as to space. The architecture serving as archetype to the cinematic revolution, of Sergei Eisenstein for example, is first of all seen as a mass, or popular, art, as opposed to art for art's sake, which Benjamin refers to as a theology of art.

Later on in the same essay, Benjamin pursues his line of reasoning: "The shooting of a film affords a spectacle unimaginable anywhere at any time before this. It represents a process which it is impossible to locate within a perspective that does not include all sorts of extraneous film accessories, such as camera equipment, lighting machinery, grips and technicians, etc. For the spectator to form an abstraction of all of that, his eye must become like the camera lens. In thus enlarging the world of objects which we maintain in the visual and auditory realm, film has resulted in a deepening of our apperception."[2]

Benjamin claims that this apperception tends to favor the mutual interpenetration of art and science. Total matter and total cinema mark the end of Quattrocento perspective. The blind alley disappears into the superimposed vision of a closed-circuit television that never turns off, that always gives and receives, directly or indirectly, all surfaces and all the pieces of a tele-topological puzzle, one in which televised permanence replaces the permanent cinema of the 1920s through the 1940s, where the public would go to forget reality just for an instant.

It is important to note here how Benjamin denies architecture its essential function of occultation; the sheltering against inclement weather also protects against all glances. For Benjamin, the architectonic no longer operates among the registers of resistance, material and appearances; it occurs now instead within the order of transparency and the ubiquity of the instantaneous, both mythical qualities that predict those of the great political and social liberation: "By close-ups we inventory the world of things around us, emphasizing the hidden details of everyday objects and exploring commonplace sites under the genial guidance of the camera. If, on the one hand, the film helps us understand the necessities of our lives, it also leads us into an immense and previously unsuspected field of action. Our shops and city streets, our offices and furnished rooms, our railroad stations and our factories seemed like prison beyond any hope of liberation. Then came the film, and with the dynamite of its tenths-of-a-second, it blew up the concentration-camp universe, so that now, abandoned in the midst of its far-flung debris, we take on adventurous expeditions. With the close-up, space expands; with slow-motion, movement takes on new dimensions. With film, we begin to see entirely new structures of matter."[3]

Gustave Flaubert had already posed the question of the multiple and of technical reproducibility when he slyly announced: "The better the telescopes, the more numerous the stars." The German philosopher was less able than the French writer to resist the delirium of interpretation. The industrial techniques at issue here entail more than the multiplication of manufactured objects or the reproduction of photographic images. We are witnessing the sudden multiplication of dimensions of matter. The industrialization of artistic "beauty," so feared by Benjamin as a consequence of darkroom technique, is doubled and intensified by the cinematic sequences of "industrialization of (scientific) truth,"[4] which apparently did not concern the philosopher a bit.

Benjamin relied on the metaphor of explosion, of the dynamiting of a town, with its debris projected over great distances. These distances, however, are no longer situated in any depth of field or "perspective." According to Benjamin, the field of action opened by cinematic technique is no longer one of urban or industrial concentration or sedentariness. We now have an open system, in which no one can find any perceptible, objective limits. It is a field of constitutive dispersal. It is a world of dispersed, or scattering, structures whose amplitude — contrary to the structuralists — we can no longer measure, structures that in a single gesture arrive at both the ancient geometric and architectonic configurations: "Just as water, gas, and electricity come into our homes from afar, responding to our needs with negligible effort," wrote Paul Valery in 1936, "so we shall be provided with visual or auditory images, which will appear and disappear at the slightest wave of the hand, hardly more than a sign." In this augury of telecommunications, the bourgeois home is merely the site of energy and other modes of supply. Its architecture is an intersection, a nodal point, a fixed pole on which inertia begins to renew the ancient sedentary ways of townspeople, legal citizens for whom the liberty to come and go is suddenly replaced by the liberation of home reception.

Elsewhere, in "Paris, Capital of the Nineteenth Century," Benjamin notes: "During this period, the office becomes the real center of gravity for the active domain of everyday life, and the de-realized individual creates a safe harbor for himself in the private home." As today we stand witness to the development of an office cosmology that is directly linked to the flowering of tele-informatics, we can attest to the accuracy of this observation which, with the accompanying decline of metropolitan sedentary behavior, affects the very structure of architecture.

The office, which was once an other-place, an architectural aside, has now become a simple screen. In the bourgeois apartment, the space reserved for work and study has become the terminal of an office-viewfinder, in which the data of tele-information instantaneously appear and disappear as the three dimensions of constructed space are translated into the two dimensions of a screen, or better of an interface, which replaces more than the volume of the ancient dwelling, with its furniture and their arrangements, its contracts and blueprints. This new arrangement also directs the more or less distant displacement of the occupant.[5] This transmutation — where the inertial confinement of the new office has become the axis of gravity and the nodal center of techno-bureaucratic society — explains yet again the contemporary, post-industrial redeployment.

With the first French experiments in "tele-labor," or long-distance work — launched in 1980 by the Direction Generale des Telecommunications — we can begin to see the real basis for this re-organization of architectural and urban space, when we begin to hear references to the "tele-local," as occurred in the multi-enterprise center directed by DATAR in Marne-la-Vallée, to the reduction of traditional office spaces, to the re-organization of employees in certain newly

73

de-centralized operations, resulting in the alleviation of investment and operational expenditures, in the renewed re-alignment of professional and family obligations, in the saving of transport time, and so forth and so on.

For telecommunications, coming together in time means, inversely, distancing oneself in space. The vast dispersion of the scattered debris now involves more than the fragments of the concentration-camp universe denounced by Benjamin. Scattered as well are the personnel, the tele-laborers, who have become objects and subjects of an energy and film transmutation whose purpose has moved from simple industrial production to the long-distance representation of that structural and post-industrial reduction that affects all neighborly relations. As Benjamin noted: "Every day, there grows a need to own the object at the closest possible proximity, through its image and even more its reproduction."[6] No longer aspects of physical space, size and proximity are now elements of the time of photographic, cinematic or infographic exposition, which is a delay of almost instantaneous response, irrespective of the distances among interlocutors.

Coming together to deconstruct structurally or to scatter to the winds, the functions here of eye and equipment become confused, since by definition the resolution of the transmitted image is its instantaneous reduction. But this reduction affects more than the simple content of representation, the projected form-image. It also takes over constructed space, the territorial form, from which emanates the organization of time through the chrono-political direction of the so-called "advanced," or developed, societies. In his memoirs,[7] Marcel Pagnol described this relationship between the eye and the equipment: "In a theater, a thousand people cannot sit in the same seat and thus we cannot say that any two of them have seen the same play. . . The playwright has to take aim at his public by taking his shotgun and firing a thousand pellets at once, if he is to strike successfully a thousand views in a single blow. Film resolves this problem, since the spectator, no matter where he is in the theater, sees exactly what the camera saw. If Charlie Chaplin looks directly into the camera, his photogram will look directly at everyone in the audience, whether they are sitting to the right or the left, in the balcony or the orchestra."

The situation of the "tele-spectator" or the "tele-laborer" at home is the same as that of the audience in the darkened theaters of Pagnol, yet with one major difference of scale, one which affects, more than the dimensions of the projection room, the space-time of the metropolitan concentration and urban sedentariness.

If the star looks directly into the camera, his "form-image" will look directly, in the televised interface, at those who are watching, whether they are in the city, suburbs or countryside, whether they are in France or elsewhere. Pagnol's movie star will be infinitely multiplied, like the stars of Flaubert's telescope.

This technical reproductivity is not exactly the same. In the case of the telescope or the cinemascope, the irruption is the same and the notion of the exactitude and resolution of the artistic image re-engages the exactitude of the form-image and the resolution of the problems of scientific observation and of experimentation in the exact sciences. As Benjamin: "The camera substitutes a space of unconscious human action for that space in which man consciously acts."

Basically, following the maxim "too much justice results in injustice," too much justness — too much exactitude in the definition of the recorded and transmitted form-image — results in inexactitude, or better, a relative uncertainty due to the interpretive delirium of the observer, be it spectator or tele-spectator. The film industry certainly knew how to use the fascination and hallucinatory character of this delirium, which remained as unclarified by the means of communication and telecommunication as by the experimentation of the exact sciences.

With this morphological and architectonic irruption, the technics of telescope and cinemascope does not give more, in that there is no real multiplication. Instead, it interrupts us differently. For the attentive observer, the slicing of physical space into different geometric dimensions, and the durable separation of geographic and constructed spaces, is replaced by the momentary break, due to the imperceptible interruption of different sequences of view-points and the perceptible interruption of broadcasting and of reception.

The new produced and projected space has less to do with lines, surfaces and volumes than with the minutiae of view-point, the dynamite of tenths-of-seconds. These view-points are simultaneously time-points in the tele-topological continuum of long-distance projection and reception.

One mode of splicing and assembling replaces another; but the untimely interference of extension and duration are far from being apprehended in any real sense, precisely because the visual unconscious intensifies, as it were, the instinctive unconscious, denounced by Freud.[8]

The inertia of tele-spectators at home has replaced the sedentary ways of the audience and the actors of the stage and streets, and precisely because the concentration in the actual time of transmission and reception has renewed the classical concentration in the actual space of cohabitation — the unity of the neighborhood, which until recently begat urban architecture.

Thus, along with the "tele-local" machinery, we find ourselves surrounded by tele-informatics equipment that memorizes the orders transmitted by travelling salespeople armed with portable terminals. It used to take two or three days for the orders to get back to the company headquarters; now it's all over in forty-five seconds. And the same goes for press journalists. The Scrib tele-editing portable terminals developed by the Bobst–Graphic company, with micro-computer screen and integrated printer, permit creation, full execution and transmission at a speed of up to thirty signals per second, which is six times faster than telex. Now, a journalist on assignment need only tap into a telephone for her or his article to pass instantaneously into the central computer at the editorial desk of the newspaper, and this at any hour of the day or night. That reporter's piece can then be typed and set automatically and without the intervention of a single employee at the printing end of the process.

In Japan, this has already happened at the level of city management, with the Mitaca experiment in the INS system — the central information agency — the inertial concentrator of facts concerning all metropolitan commercial and industrial residents, users, equipment and enterprises. According to official Japanese government statements, if this experiment in the city of Mitaca works, if this process of instantaneous informational capitalization of an entire city proves successful, it could be extended to Tokyo, Osaka, Nagoya and finally to the fifty largest cities of Japan.

This view of telematic and megalopolitan management seems to have found a supporter, recently, in the person of maritime ecologist Jacques Cousteau. According to Cousteau, in the year 2000 Paris will have to be "a federation of villages in which communication will occur through video rather than physical transport of people." It is as if naval strategy served as model and reference for territorial management. Or else it is as if telecommunication's "populating of time" — such as vacations, interruptions, and so forth — suddenly replaced all the ancient cohabitations, the populating of space, the actual urban proximity.

⊛   ⊛   ⊛

Bonhoeffer once wrote: "In its form, creation faced God in an altogether new manner, and, in this face-to-face encounter, creation belonged to Him completely." Now — with the opto-electronic ubiquity and its incidence over the configuration of territory — we can revise this statement, as regards the teletopological metamorphoses of the city: "in its form-image, creation faces man in an altogether new manner, and, in this interface, creation appears to belong to *him* completely." It must go without saying that this term "completely" is an optical illusion, a simultaneously energy- and film-derived illusion. From this we get the term electronic optic, an optic that no longer results from the properties of additional glass lenses. Rather, electronic optics results from properties of instantaneous electronic transmission, from the transparence of distances which renews not only the physical appearances of materials but also the morphological and architectonic configuration of the human environment.

We are no longer primarily concerned with the displacement — or with our being displaced — in the space of a passage. We are now involved with the dephasing in time of the instant of a disjunction–conjunction. This is a concurrence of technical circumstances in which appearances are all against us, all precisely against us in the opto-electronic interface. The separation of different sites in the original geopolitics of the rural, the communal, the urban and the national, has become the interruption of the non-site of contemporary chrono-politics.

This intermittent structuring of duration — like that of physical extension — by systems of interlocution and by interruption of communications, though radically different from that of the parcelling of land, is nevertheless equally concerned with spatial arrangements, with the ripping to pieces of real estate, the irruption in which the architectonic undergoes a series of topological distortions whose effects still remain largely unknown. To this end, consider the history of architectonic elements, such as walls, doors, windows, chimneys. The first window is the door, the door-window necessary for access to and thus for the reality of the home, since we could not conceptualize a house without some means of access.

In the first dwellings, the illuminating opening did not exist. There was an entrance and sometimes a chimney of some sort. The window as such — the second window — appeared fairly late, in the sites of monastic cults, before becoming popular among the rural homes and only then, and especially, in the palace and the homes of the bourgeoisie.

The third window is a recent invention: the television screen, a removable and portable window that opens onto the false day of the speed of light emissions. The television screen is an introverted window, one which no longer opens onto adjoining space but instead faces beyond the perceptible horizon. Thus, if the door-window constitutes an opening — a threshold for the immediate and undifferentiated access of people, things, daylight and direct vision, as well as a form of ground-level ventilation that works with the more elevated ventilation of the chimney — then the specialized window is more selective, because it interrupts the passage of bodies. The specialized window is a puncture, a mediated opening for solar light and nearby perspectives. In this context the TV screen becomes a selector of electronic images, an audio-visual medium for the indirect light of the cathode tube.

While the door is both the origin of the necessarily penetrable dwelling and of the specialized window, it is also the first piece of furniture, since it is the same vertically and horizontally. The drawbridge is an example, as is a sluice gate, or the back panel of a cart. Each is a kind of door that itself transports, inside or out, in the coming and going, which illustrates precisely the turning motion of the revolving door, the first technical vehicle of the nineteenth-century domicile, awaiting the elevator.

The automobile door thus constitutes the second door, but as a door of a doorway outside of the walls, it also completes the distortion effect of the screen of the third window. As a means of physical and communicative access over great distances, the audiovisual and automotive media merge here, collapsing the traditional architectonic structure. Basically, just as the television set posted before the sofa is an object that punctures the walls, the garage must also be considered in the context of its effect on the rooms of the house. Both are thresholds of transformation that provoke the anamorphosis of constructed architectural and urban structures. Movable elements — such as seats, beds or various arrangements — conspire with new means of transportation and telecommunication to contribute to the deterioration of a stability which is actually a stasis of immobile equilibrium. As a phenomenon of accelerated substitution, contemporary living becomes the crossroads for mass-media. At this point, the garage could easily replace the house, that "dwelling" which was only a parking lot for the nomad's furniture anyway.

Will we soon replace the ensemble of apartment furniture with active and dynamic vectors that will themselves progressively but radically modify the configuration of the building, and then of architectural morphology? Hasn't the automobile already become a detachable part of the floor plan, the necessary condition for the appearance of the secondary residence, the detachable habitat of the principle residence? Aren't we witnessing here, in the development of the automotive dwellingplace, a repetition of those architectonic elements already noted earlier? Having made the window autonomous through the television screen, and the door through the automobile, will we now participate in the complete disintegration of the building? Don't we already feel a kind of domiciliary atopia in the urban absorption of towns and suburbs? Isn't the ostensibly functional development of the modern architectural plan, with its hierarchies of space into principal and secondary rooms or receiving and serving units, really nothing more than an aspect of the different modes of access, such as door, window, stair, elevator, as well as of the means of automotive communication and audiovisual telecommunication? As regards recent developments in advanced technologies, we must pose one final question. How will it end?

Here, the video-cassette recorder affords us — in the wake of telescopes and cinemascopes — a new aspect of the mutation in progress, one whose supremacy is already in the works, with the arrival of a new type of inertia in which the building will once again recover all its reality.

We know the primordial role of the measure of time in the history of all societies, from the early religious and political calendars, the *clepsydra*, the sundial, the clock, down to the present digital ticking of the quartz watch. With the video-cassette recorder, with its pre-recorded tapes, or better its differentiated re-transmissions, we still have an organization of time, an electronic calendar done in advance that participates in the management of time, but now of a time that has not yet arrived.

The advanced technologies advance into time in order to create day, a supplementary "false day." On the one hand there is the primary day, wherein we live; on the other is the secondary day, which is recorded somewhere for us. Just as the secondary residence exists by means of the automotive mode of communication, this secondary, supplementary day occurs thanks to audiovisual modes of telecommunication.

This stereophonic and stereoscopic doubling of space and time offers multiple correspondences between the differentiated residence and the differentiated re-transmission of the advanced video technologies. In the one, the heat is turned on electrically to prepare for the weekend, while in the other the timer is set automatically, and electronically, so as to record things that will be seen much later. If we tried to figure the damage to the environment over the last twenty years caused by the multiplication of supplementary residences used for only a few days at a time, we would also have to attempt to estimate the effects of that curious phenomenon of temporal anticipation. This would be made all the more difficult since we have always underestimated the importance of the day and of daylight on territorial organization and administration. This importance comes not only from the alternation of night and day, but also from a system of interruptions of activities which structured the life of former societies and the administration of their different environments. Basically, time is lived — physiologically, sociologically and politically — to the extent that it is interrupted.

While, perhaps, continuous time is that of chronology or history, it certainly is not that of everyday experience. Interruptions of activity or productivity are essential to the structuring of real time, for individuals and for social groups, and here the day is the reference point and the primary standard for these structuring interruptions, as is evidenced in common expressions such as "to see the light of day" or "to call it a day." More than any other physical, urban, or architectonic barrier, and more than any other natural or political border, the day marks off differences of temporality, differences of regimes that affect the consciousness of time passing, not only through the rhythms of sleeping and waking but more with the eternal return of daylight and of night.

Thus, the region and the city are not organized exclusively through a cadastral system of blocks, neighborhoods, city-centers and peripheries, or clusters of apartment complexes. They are also arranged through a calendar system of vacations, leaves-of-absence, and holidays off. Some interruptions return us to the religious purposes of the Sabbath or the Sunday rest, the seventh day of Creation, a vacation dedicated to contemplation, to the reception of the finished product. Others, such as the lock-out and the strike, are interruptions of production that are also necessary to reflection and to a dialogue among social partners or antagonists.

Today, technology plays an analogous role in creating from all forms of new interruptions a modification of time, a distortion of the astronomical day which affects the arrangement of urban space and of architecture, as the window displaces the door.

The solar day that structured the living day was displaced by the chemical day, in which candlelight permitted the development of numerous nocturnal activities. The chemical day gave way to the electric day, which indefinitely prolonged the perception of daylight. With the recent advent of the electronic day, the extension of day and of visibility spreads, taking over space as the extension of an audio-visual and tele-topological continuum, and erasing all the antipodes — those of geographic distances, as well as the dead angles of that domain constructed by closed-circuit TV.

This sudden distortion of the visibility of daylight is more than the simple consequence of televisual technologies capable of turning space in on itself. It also involves techniques of aerospatial communication, which are themselves capable of twisting the length of the astronomic day. For example, returning from San Francisco to Europe, we can follow an aerial line that passes over the glaciers of Greenland. If we do so, at certain periods of the year, we participate in an extraordinary phenomenon: there is no night. Behind us glow the red fires of dusk and, in the same instant, ahead of us glimmer the green lights of dawn.

Seeing that which had previously been invisible becomes an activity that renews the exoticism of territorial conquests of the past. But seeing that which is *not really* seen becomes an activity that exists for itself. This activity is not exotic but *endotic,* because it renews the very conditions of perception, which is necessary to physical reality. Thus, the invention — twenty years ago — of holography, appears as a metaphor for advanced technologies. Holography is in no way the perfection of perspective, nor is it the most perfect accomplishment of relief and of stereoscopic vision. It is instead the end: the extermination of all perspective reality.

What is false, then, is not only the accelerated perspective, the anamorphosis; it is depth itself, the physical and geophysical distance in time. We see this everywhere: in supersonic transports, in laser optics, in recent developments in holographic film and three-dimensional television. With this invention of a day defined by technological speed, in direct opposition to astronomical time, the primary question becomes less one of relations to *history* than one of relations to *time* , and to the regimes of temporality that issue forth from advanced technologies. In this environment, in which all appearances are against us, the metamorphoses of acceleration contribute to the deformation of ancient reference points, such as physical standards and other architectural archetypes. Basically, reality encounters the fate of modernity: it has always already happened.

The moment of the direct perception of objects, surfaces and natural or constructed volumes gives way to the indirect and mediated reception, an interface that avoids day-to-day duration, as well as the calendar of everyday living. We will never be neighbors in any televisual proximity, and the media are not our contemporaries. We live today in an ever-growing fault between the promptness of the broadcasts and our own capacity to grasp and measure the present moment. The question of *modernity* and *post-modernity* is superseded by that of *reality* and *post-reality:* we are living in a system of technological temporality, in which duration and material support have been supplanted as criteria by individual retinal and auditory instants.

The perspectival effects of classical ornaments and the cinematic characteristics of certain styles, such as baroque, liberty or neo-liberty, is replaced by an integral cinematism, an absolute transitivity, involving the complete and thorough decomposition of realty and property. This decomposition is urban, architectural, and territorial. It is based on the deterioration of the ancient primacy of the physical separation and spatial limitation of human activities. And this very deterioration occurs so as to facilitate the interruption and commutation of time — or better, the absence of time — in instantaneous intercommunication.

It is as if we were directly participating in a transformation that will reach every constitutive component of the constructed environment. Meanwhile, we are waiting for an atopia which will do to architectural domiciliation what decentralization and suburbanization have done to the City. Something will affect the building in its very persistence, the resistance of its materials, the duration of its immediate efficiency. It will become less than a decor — a form-image as unreliable as a mirage.

⊛　⊛　⊛

"An image perfect for all speeds would be fantastic, one would suppose."

This commercial slogan for a German VHS — which extends Walter Benjamin's view on the nature of architecture — also illustrates the end of the classical optical perspective: the arrival of an opto-electronic pseudo-perspective, a (fantastic) accelerated perspective, one ruled less by the vanishing point than by the simultaneous vanishing of *all* points, and of all instants, in a transmission in which all points without any dimension (pixels) and all instants without any perceptible duration compose an image whose formal perfection springs not from an optic convergence but from a commutation of various forms of information. In this world, the speed of electronic propagation is suddenly the equivalent of an ocular stability, which itself replaces, in the cathode interface, the ancient statics of materials.

Since what we see comes from that which is not apparent, the immaterial character of the emergence of televised forms mixes up certain aspects of metaphysics.[10] Further, with the fall of the advertising slogan — "one would think" — the problem of seeing as thinking is once more posed. With visibility as the foundation for construing belief as ocular or optic, and as the basis for moral, ethical and scientific validity, we are once more at the level of the theological debate that emanated from Galileo's telescope: "Can we say we have actually taken part in a Mass that was seen through a telescopic lens?" What seemed before an overly scrupulous Jesuit quibble now becomes a question of reality — or post-reality — that concerns instruments of measure and communication, as well as architecture.

In 1979, for example, former zoo director and video cameraman Jean-Paul Pouvreau and B. Devaux, director of traveling shows and animal films, proposed to abolish zoos in order to end the suffering of incarcerated animals. They suggested replacing live animals with tele-visual images that would be shown in a video-zoo without animals, installed in a space of 2000 to 3000 square meters. With the help of video-informatics arranging the space of an electronically programmed projection that would integrate, in a noctarium, the sequence of day and night for the natural environments of exposed, and over-exposed, fauna, these two created, in broad strokes, the means by which architecture would become no more than the scaffolding for an artificial environment, one whose physical dimensions have become instantaneous opto-electronic information.

We know this video-city, this televisual urbanization predicted by these two ecologists and suggested, for Europeans, by the experience of Atlanta, where, since 1980, Ted Turner's Cable News Network has allowed Americans to receive at home and direct — 24 hours a day and seven days a week, every day and every week — images from around the world through a broadcast satellite orbiting above the Equator.[11] Peacefully seated in their white clapboard homes with wraparound porches, at the crossroads of the Great Plains of the Middle West, the viewers of Cable News Network can leisurely watch the cars that pass before their homes or the television scoops from Iran, Iraq and other so-called hot spots. In this encounter — permitted by the artificed view from the cathode window — the third dimension trembles, and the third mode of dividing space becomes insufficient. Where once the distance of time was disrupted by the velocity vector of instantaneous transmissions, now the very nature of the environment is subjected to electronic fadings and parasitic scoops. The former televised daily news has been replaced by the permanence and direct exclusivity that create for CNN viewers a continuous televisual day, encased in the meteorology of a visual day, just as television sequences are ensconced in the monitors of a video control-booth.

We have passed beyond caring about the supremacy of one mode of information over the press, radio or film. Our house has become a press house, an architecture in which the information-dimension grows and intensifies, and in direct opposition to the activities of all journalists. The contour of daily living and the framing of viewpoint in an architectonic constructed of doors and doorways, windows and mirrors are replaced by a cathode framework, an indirect opening in which the electronic false-day functions like a camera lens, reversing the order of appearances to the benefit of an imperceptible transparence, and submitting the supremacy of certain constructive elements to that cathode window that rejects both the portal and the light of day.

Camera obscura, planetarium, noctarium: in these, architecture recovers its obscure origins. If the photo or film studio began somewhere in the cave of the philosophers, the crypt of the cenotaphs and the darkroom of the perspectivists, today it threatens and takes over the integrity of the visible continuum, changing sensible appearances into so many instances, mere specters of a perceptive and perspective reality about to disappear.

We can measure and record the evolution of this disappearance by considering the history and archaeology of shadow theaters. These began with the eighteenth-century fondness for optical and scientific curios. One such was the *eidophusicon* that appeared in London in 1781. It was a set piece painted in three dimensions, and lit so as to give the illusion of actual depth. In 1792, Robert Barker offered the first panorama and, in Paris in 1822, Daguerre invented the diorama. Finally, on December 28, 1895, the Lumière brothers conducted their first moving-picture show, in the basement of the Grand Cafe on the Boulevard des Capucines.

In all of these, we study the diverse projection apparatuses—magic lanterns, the *phenascitiscope,* the kinetoscope, and all the cinemascopes — and the accompanying architecture of the first projection rooms — such as the cylindrical form of the panoramas, the spheres, and the rotundas that prefigure, in the nineteenth century, Jeaulme's Panorama, or hemispheric cinema, and even the space of integrated holography—in order to envision the transformations of the constructed environment in the face of telecommunications developments, such as the use of satellites and fiber-optic cable networks.

Why have historians focused on the iron and glass architecture of Paxton's 1851 Crystal Palace, ignoring the architecture of light of the darkrooms of the same period? On the one hand, the development of transparence was established as a result of the materiality of large surfaces of glass, held up by an impressing array of metal scaffolding. On the other hand, transparence entered secretly in the unnoticed architectonic mutation of a wall-screen. The images on this wall increasingly assumed the value of space, taking over all the dimensions in the projection room, and finally fusing and confusing architecture with projection technique — a fusion that had previously eluded the fresco, the mosaic and the stained glass, for those methods of representation relied on daylight that slipped through the architectural openings.

Whereas the figures of representation used to appear in the solar light, or else in the luminosity of a flame, such as the flickering chiaroscuro of candelabras, today they appear (and disappear) by means of the electronic light of instantaneous representation which controls the lighting of built structures, as well as the diverse sources of complementary, artificial light. Preferring shadow and obscurity, a new horizon is revealed, a negative horizon which relies, not on the direct visibility of night and day, but rather on a false day of indirect visibility — one which has no relationship whatsoever to the lighting of the building, which used to be a necessary pre-condition for the art of construction.

The foyer, as the fireplace, was once a decisive element in the traditional home. Conceptually, it now suffers a strange fate: the foyer of heat is separated from that of light. The optic foyer first began with Clausewitz' metaphoric use of the powers of projection of additional concave and convex lenses: "As the rays of the sun united in the foyer of the concave mirror and, forming a perfect image, produce there the maximum incandescence, the energies and contingencies of war united in the principle battle, and produce there a supreme and concentrated effect."

Clausewitz's foyer will find its autonomy in Edison's electric bulb, and then even more in the terminal of all natural illumination, that place of electronic light. In that light of speed, the German advertising agency will produce a jingle repeating the metaphoric arguments of the Prussian military strategist.

Behind the expression *a perfect image,* the essence of

representation, which is its technique, does not give us more; it interrupts us in a different way. We need no longer hide the occultation and interruption that only served the ends of demonstrating and promoting different techniques, including those of architecture and urban development. The apparent multiplication of optic and video performances always hides a subtraction, since the representation is never more than one single reduction among many possibilities.

If architecture offers a view through the very materiality of the erection of walls, partitions and buildings, it also contributes to the dissimulation of the horizon of appearances. In this, architecture operates in a manner similar to the way in which state-of-the-art technologies of communication make prisons more visible and more shadowy.

More than any form of demonstration, it is this occultation that is the common denominator of all technologies, old or new. It is the privileged analyst of all arrangements of space and time. For example, the first tableau, the first means of ocular representation, was the opening for doorways and windows. This was long before the easel-and-canvas painting, which so often was self-enclosed, as in a triptych. To understand the first tableau, we would have to try to return to the visual unconscious, to the nature of the opening and the closing, rather than attempt to repeat individual demonstrative performances of one electronic optic or another.

To this end, consider the evolution and three-dimensional extension of the light-providing opening from the ancient cloister, through the mullion windows of the Middle Ages, the great lancet and rose windows, past the special effects of gothic architecture, to the bow-windows and the great metal spokes of the last century and beyond, and up to the glass facades of our present skyscrapers, and the curtain-walls that were themselves contemporaries to the invention and development of the cathode opening. All of this helps explain the importance of this transmutation of appearances, the subsequent supremacy of the televisual window over the door and other traditional means of access, a supremacy that already contributes to the decline of public space and the decrease of collective venues.

There are fewer theaters, grand performance spaces (such as opera and symphony halls), stadiums and other places for the effective, collective and simultaneous presence of large numbers of spectators. This reduction comes from direct and global-vision broadcasting, which devalues the real presence of thousands and even tens of thousands of people. As ticket prices and profits have given way to the exorbitant fees the networks are willing to pay for exclusive broadcast rights, we have arrived at a point in which some are seriously contemplating completely eliminating the crowds from all major sporting events, and simply televising the matches and games in empty stadiums, filled with nothing but advertising billboards.

In the United States, where sports are important, cable networks have offered new basketball teams to make up the difference caused by the disappearance of their spectators. This deregulation of public space in the service of household reception is in every point analogous to airline deregulation, to the deregulation of American railroads, and especially of AMTRAK between 1960 and 1975, which affected both the demography and the social class of passengers. Deregulation reduced transport delays from the East Coast to the West, as it also devastated passenger airlines— as had already happened to the general infrastructure of the rail system, including stations, siding, tracks, and so forth.

Once again we encounter the decisive importance of speed in the disqualification of old vehicles and, even more, of an entire environment, such as Formula I racetracks and stadiums, that fall victim to instantaneous broadcast, with the inevitable impact of direct television on the habitat, on the nature of neighborhood relationships and on the entire urban infrastructure. Once again, the subsequent use of geostationary satellites to assure urban and inter-urban tele-communication, in Brazil for example, relocates the center of the city, ripping it from the belfry of the town hall and hanging it instead from the zenith of some satellite in high orbit over the earth.

"Immediacy is a fraud," wrote Bonhoeffer in the early thirties, at the exact moment in which radio, telephone and other new modes of mass communication enabled Adolf Hitler to establish control over Germany. We can now measure the perverse effects of this fraud by observing that that which is present and shared is today discredited by the immediacy of that which is not. When a CB hacker explains that his radio allows him to speak "with people he doesn't know, and to communicate beyond the circle of geographic affinities," this means that that which is *not there* controls from long distances that which is present.

Finally, this "pressure of the audiovisual," comprised of the disruptive influences of instantaneous broadcast on our political and other habits, is merely an expression of the deterioration of the unity of the neighborhood, and the subsequent dissolution of the politics of territorial arrangement, as exemplified by the universalization of the *barrios,* homelands, *favelas* and other worker-ghettos of the Third World. Thus, the insidious discredit cast for the last twenty years over *geopolitical extensivity* in favor of a *transpolitical intensivity* of exchange and communication resulted in the progressive decline of the national State, shredded by the demands for internal autonomy and the opposing economic and strategic requirements for international alliances. Despite the illusion of multinational corporations and international marketplaces, the deregulation of different organizational and governmental systems resulted in the reversal of the aggregative, federal principle. This propitious dissociation assumed the aspect of a decentralization that was, in fact, nothing more than the prolongation of decolonization. From this emerged an infinite series of fracture lines, divorces and cleavages — all in the name of various liberties — that divided ethenes, groups, classes, and social partners, all the way up to the largest national or international communal entities, so as to create an administration of time, a "chronopolitical" management of activities that challenges the traditional geopolitical arrangement, re-ordering the very forms of population and, with those, urban architecture itself.

We saw this kind of deconstruction and morphological irruption of architecture in the earlier emergence of metallic structures at the London and Paris World's Fairs: the accrued transparency of appearances, the residual character of an industrial construction that was already nothing more than a scaffolding for glass but also — with that recuperated supremacy of light over matter — the devaluation of stone, the decline of dense materials for facades and partitions, the rise of the structuralism of the curtain wall.

In the nineteenth century, an anonymous author described the Crystal Palace: "We see a trellis of lines of exquisite subtlety, but there is no index that allows us to appreciate its true dimensions and distances, and so the eye slides along the length of an infinite perspective that loses itself in the mist." Herein is announced in advance the crisis of physical dimensions, the advent of buildings stripped of any optic center, in which the structural architectonic of iron and glass behaves as the later image-form will behave in the computer terminals and the televised sequences. In the new trellis of lines, 625 or 819 lines, of imperceptible subtlety, the *pixel* replaces the bolt and rivet. The eye of the telespectator slides along the length of an infinite electronic perspective, and the architecture of light becomes nothing more than the computer's memory — a sequential, modular or matrix system that was prefigured by the first metallic structures, the optic theaters and other panoramas of the nineteenth century.

In the same way, the World's Fairs of the Belle Epoque anticipated this agglomeration without agglomeration. In this universal over-exposure of commercial and cultural exchanges, the City progressively lost its authenticity as the unity of time and place for an effective cohabitation in the face of an accelerated de-urbanization. With the disruptions in the nature of territorial population — through decolonization and decentralization — the traditional sedentary life gave way to a confinement that resulted from advanced technologies. In the establishment of this inertial confinement, the basis was no longer the geometric axes of the urban arrangement, nor the geomorphological centrality of the group of villages. Instead, the new order relied on the accrued polarization of exchanges and activities, a temporal, nodal, polarization in which the interlocution and interruption of a momentary sitting, little by little, supplanted the older network of highway communication and railyard turntable.

The antique, cadastral segregation of provinces and neighborhoods gave way to time management, in which individualities would become progressively sharper, what with the risks of conflicts and the internecine struggles built into this sort of situation. Now, with the decline of the concrete presence of users, we can no longer easily verify the devaluation of the *close* and the *nearby* to the exclusive advantage of the *distant*. This is the presence of absence, whose unlimited abundance is revealed by the new means of instantaneous inter-communication, such as telematics, citizen-band radio, walkman and other video-technologies.

ⓐ ⓐ ⓐ

Alongside the transformation of human populations due to the domestication of fire, water, and wind, alongside the transmutations of the natural and constructed environment provoked by new modes and sources of energy, can we now add the impact of new kinds of information, and of a sudden metropolitan tele-distribution?

We already know the evolution visited upon the rural landscape by the distribution of electricity, as well as the rail and road transport systems. We also already know the mutations undergone by the urban landscape, thanks to the elevator and the subway, and, of course, we can look out the window and see the influence of new energy sources — such as solar energy — on our patterns of habitation. And, if we already know all of these, isn't it about time we began to wonder about the relationships between these new energy systems and those new modes of mass communication? Systems theory has long demonstrated the logic of flow for transport and transmission, the visible or invisible dry fluxes of a "substance," generally without consistency, but with great consequences.

If *informatics* — with its networks, memory banks and terminals — is actually a kind of *energetics,* an energy form, then transmitted information becomes a mode of formation that affects for now and into the foreseeable future all the different types of arrangements we have been considering. Where once the old energy sources of coal, gas, oil, and electricity gave rise to a longlasting and continuous current of transformation (although for a shorter period than similar ones of the past), the energy of information feeds inversely an alternative, extremely brief, discontinuous current of transformation, in which the rule of space and of the spatiality of extension of different rural and urban places gives way to temporality, and the nature of regimes of temporalities, produced by advanced technologies.

From this new order comes what we consider to be the essential notions of the *direct* and the *deferred.* In the same instant, we see the philosophic inversion of the relationship of substance to accident, linked to the soaring of a kind of energetism that itself emerges from the catastrophic performances of nuclear technologies. The new primacy of an accident — conceived in all of its instantaneous, energetic power — is no longer thought of as some sort of deformation, some kind of destructive danger. Instead it becomes a formation, a productive and constructive probability. Instead of relying on the formal or dialectic logic of the past, this new formation relies on the paradoxical logic that — through industrial and scientific practices — prolongs the crisis of determinism, the popular "uncertainty principle" of contemporary physics.

In this "energetism" that emerges from quantum mechanics, the accident is no longer that of a visible dislocation: a substantively constituted ensemble, the apparent irruption of some kind of object. It is instead the inapparent rupture of the unity of measure, be it of matter, light, space or time. It is a transference accident that challenges all primary references — such as the unity of place and time — in favor of the motion of motion: that absolute transitivity of speed that is to time as it was to space just yesterday, in the heyday of Einstein's relativist continuum.

Until the end of the nineteenth century, space — in the distinction of movements and of physical and geographical extension — acted as the differentiation between space and time. At the turn of the century, with Albert Einstein, we begin to see a preliminary confusion of terms and appearances; space becomes space / time, in a spatio-temporal continuum. This great telescoping of two variables becomes a mere disturbance when considered in the context of our present fragmentation, disintegration of dimensions, and quantum indeterminacy, all of which are borne of that fusion in which relativist space-time, and its quadri-dimensional continuum, vanish before the emergence of a dimensionless space-speed, a kind of discontinuum in which the grandeur of speed surges like some primitive space: the standard for all dimensions, precisely because geometry has revealed that — in the abstract extension — all measurements can be considered measures of length, wave lengths.

Speed is thus no longer simply a measurable qualitative dimension, as it was in Einstein's relativist system, where "acceleration is defined as the quotient of an infinitely small increase in speed and by the correspondent increase in time."[12] Speed has become a qualitatively measured space, whose dimensions are based on the constant of light, of the light-standard and only the light-standard. It seems imprecise to continue to claim, as do some scientists like Carl Sagan, that "speed expands time in the instant in which it shrinks space." Acceleration does not really reduce space, nor does it really stretch time, because, since the invention of the field — as in the gravitational and electromagnetic fields — those two spatio-temporal variables are now perceived as "accidental" and statistical rather than "substantial."

According to Einstein: "With the invention of the electromagnetic field, a daring imagination was needed to fully comprehend that it was not the conduct of bodies but rather the conduct of something that existed between them, *i.e.* the field, that could be the essential for ordering and interpreting all events."[13] At the end of his life, Einstein refused to write about these atomic and quantum events as "occurring in space and time . . . "

According to Epicurus, "time is the accident of accidents." With this in mind, we can say that the space-time of the Einsteinian relativist continuum was the accident of accidents, of the transfer of speed. In this, the speed of light illuminated matter in the instant in which light offered a representation, but a hyper-cinematic representation, devoid of all physical dimensions, which, after the downfall of ether, already predicted the field. Maxwell's equations finally passed from the field of philosophical and theoretical representation into the field of atomic and quantum action, in which the classical depth of field of Einstein's relativist continuum begins to blur, just like that of the Quattrocento perspectivists.

We can see this situation today in the most recent audiovisual technologies. Having witnessed the advent of television, cinemascope, high-fidelity, all the way up to the recent experiments with hemispheric cinema (and again, in 1982 at the Collége de France, with integrated holographic film), we now see that every venture — irrespective of the sophistication of the means employed to create a kind of visual or aural relief — is bound to fail. This built-in failure does not arise from the quality of the acoustic enclosure, nor from the properties of the specified optics. It comes from *habit* — from our own system of habit — because with custom this so-called "relief" becomes integrated and then disappears, regardless of its original verisimilitude.

Basically, according to all reports, after only a few months the imaginary third dimension becomes blurred, and soon no one can tell the difference in depth between the photogram and the hologram. It's as if the fourth dimension was the only relief, and the solitary depth a depth of time which we never really get used to, a paroptic depth which allows us to see a day which is not exactly that of solar or any other light. Instead, we see by means of a subliminary illumination, and one which has no relationship whatsoever with dimensions, distances, or the depths of the traditional field of space.

Commutation has progressively replaced the limitation and interfacing of surface; instantaneous reception has replaced departure, in the inertia of a confinement that is becoming the norm. All of this has happened because the habitual notions of height, length and width have undergone a transmutation, one that affects the organization of ocular and auditory perception, and thus the entire administration of territories and of all construction. Now one architectonic element stands ready to supplant all others. The window replaces the door.

This is an event of considerable importance. It reaches to the heart and soul, the principle and nature of architecture; it relegates the protocol of physical access — as well as the necessity of an effective presence — to a secondary plane of actual experience.

We can now better understand the precise materiality of architecture which fascinated Walter Benjamin. It was connected less to the walls, floors, and opacity of surfaces than to the primacy of the access protocol of doors and bridges, but it also referred equally to the ports and other means of transport, that prolonged the nature of the threshold, the practical function of the entryway. This protocol of physical access gave all its meaning to the space of a dwelling and of a City; both were linked to the primacy of the sedentary over the nomadic ways of our origins. And all of this is being swept away by advanced technologies, especially those of domestic teledistribution.

The cathode window and the matrix screen are able to displace doors and physical means of communication, because cinematic representation has already displaced the reality of the effective presence, the real presence of people and things. Further, the accident of instantaneous transfer machinery displaces the substance of space-time, in favor of a kind of energy reduction and a hyper-cinematic reductionism that affects urbanism and architecture, but above all else re-orders geometry and the dimensions of physical space.

With all of this, there is no reason to stand stunned before post-modern facades or the ambiguous character of an architecture that has announced its own superficiality. The mediating of the environment now affects much more than simply the tools of communication, such as control towers, video-based management, nodal centers, and informatics centers; it has come to re-order intimate space, the very nature of our domiciles, through the development of teledistribution.

Servan-Schreiber's apartment offers a taste of this future; every room save the bedroom is dominated by a piece of advanced electronic furniture. There's a telex-computer console for satellite correspondence, a game computer for the kids, a home-management computer for domestic affairs, an educational computer for the study of languages, history or math, a word-processor replacing the old typewriter, not to mention televisions and VCR's.

These performances and electronic video-performances are matched only by the architectural nullity of all buildings. This is the nullity we see in the arrangement of Silicon Valley, the electronic suburb of an agglomeration without agglomeration. We have arrived, in the era of telematic non-separability, at the zero degree of architecture.

4

The Lost Dimension

Jorge-Luis Borges once remarked, "If something were unforgettable, we could never think of anything else."

Essentially, *memory* — electronic or other — is a fixation. This fixation becomes neurotic or pathological if not accompanied by the projectile capacities of the imaginary, whose very possibility requires forgetting, understood as the absence of reminiscence. In the same way, a momentary absence of consciousness, a picnoleptic interruption, is the existential prerequisite for time, and for the identity of time as lived by individuals. In a parallel manner, the absence of the dimension of the point, or punctum, that iconic cutting of the representation of physical dimensions, is the basis for the appearance of a geometrical configuration inherited from the past. This brings us to a re-consideration of Henri Poincaré's analysis of continuity and discontinuity.

According to Poincaré, if physical dimensions could be legitimately considered as slices in a continuum — perceived as absolute and necessary, in the manner of all substance — couldn't we also equally legitimately consider the absence of consciousness, the picnoleptic cut, as a dimension of time, a dimension of that "depth of time" that no longer concerns itself with the indispensable accounting of the effects of observation on the observed processes, thereby contributing to the renewal of the experience of space and duration?

As I have explained elsewhere,[1] the picnoleptic absence reveals a state of rapid wakefulness that is inversely proportional to the state of rapid, or paradoxical, sleep that produces dream images. This confirms our sense that acceleration and deceleration, or the movement of movement, are the only true dimensions of space, of speed-space, of dromospheric space.

This space is not defined as substantive or extensive; it is not primarily volume, mass, larger or smaller density, extension, nor longer, shorter, or bigger superficie. It is first and foremost *accidental* and *intensive*. Its intensity, be it small or big, is not measured according to the portion, proportion, dimension, or cutting of some morphological, Euclidean or non-Euclidean continuum. Its intensity is measured instead by change of speed, a change that instantaneously produces a change of light and of representation.

We now have a different day. Instead of a solar or otherwise illuminated day, we have a subliminary and para-optic day that has no relationship whatsoever to direct observation, and in which representations and configurations arise less from the separation of the points, lines, and planes of visual experience, or image resolution, than from the interruption of projection sequences. The projection of the light of speed, which is paradoxical light, constructs the dimensions of our fields of action and of perception, fields in which the action is no longer separated from its representation, and so the gap between world time and human time ends. The relativist notions of length of speed and depth of time finally allow us to understand the paradox of non-separability of events.[2]

Speaking in an interview about his recent book, *Time and Narrative,* Paul Ricoeur noted, "We are not capable of producing a concept of time that is at once cosmological, biological, historical and individual." In this, Ricoeur ignores the contributions of science and technology, as well as the decisive importance of speed in the new conceptions of time.

He also ignores the nature of technological narratives. For example, when the philosopher explains, "The activity of the narrative consists in constructing coherent temporal ensembles: in order to configure time," he is describing more than the human sciences. In fact, above all else, he is expressing the situation of the exact sciences: the production regimes of temporalities by means of primary and advanced technologies. As already noted, these coherent temporal assemblages contribute to the configuration of space and time, of individual time, of the social time of the history of mentalities, and — first and foremost — the scientific and political time of physics, geophysics and astrophysics.

Do we represent the construction, or construct the representation? This question lies at the heart of debates concerning the new alliance of the sciences, arts and technologies,[3] as well as debates about the role of computers in conception and construction. Einstein wrote, "There is no scientific truth." From that point on, we have but momentary representations, whose sequences constantly accelerate to the point at which we lose our grasp of any solid reference or marker, except, that is, for the quantum of action in theoretical physics and the punctum of practical representation.

But, to return to Borges, if forgetting is indispensable to the projectivity of imagination and the propagation of thought, the point is a point of reference of geometric projectivity only to the extent that it is a gap or lack, an absence of dimension, a black hole. As an obscurity, the point is as necessary to the revelation of physical appearances as the darkroom is to the objective appearances in photography and of the cinematographic photogram. The same could be said for film pigments, and the pixels of telematic images. Thus, the point is that lost dimension that allows us to recuperate ourselves: that bug, that micro-processor of our mathematical and esthetic representation and our temporal and spatial configurations.

The subsequent loss of the machine — or, better, loss of the dimensional mechanics spawned by ancient Greek geometry — is no great loss. As Mandelbrot has noted,[4] we are only losing a certain relationship of conformity, such as entity, unity and symmetry, that came from a long ago past.[5] In this, the Aristotelian privilege of substance over accident,[6] and of duration over instantaneity, was maintained, so that temporality was perceived as linear; and so the equivalence of speeds and distances had to grow progressively strained.

Finally, *informatics* now appears, as a kind of *energetics*, as a mode of formation, because the punctum of electronic action is virtually or practically instantaneous. If, according to computer assisted conceptualizations, accident has become the probable imminence,[7] the point, the pixel, is the imminence of physical dimensions, the accident of the transfer of the traced, as of all surface or volume projectivity. Thus, if the "man-machine" interface is the product of electronic interactivity combined with relativist non-separability, then the synthetic image is the visible consequence of a static conception of real time and real space. This purely theoretical and quantitative conception finds its apparent, practical confirmation in the appearance and disappearance of those form-images composed of points without dimension and instants without duration, digitally controlled by the algorithms of an encoded language.

This energetic formation, as informatic generation, is no longer confined to computer-generated images of synthesis. It now involves the configuration of production and the final arrangement of products, which can be verified as much in "computer-assisted information" (CAI) and "computer-assisted production" (CAP) as in the structure of the highest performance vehicles and equipment. At Matra's military division, for example, since 1980 an increasingly intimate bond has developed between CAI and CAP. This relationship involves Euclid Vax 780 computers linked together by a Decnet system. These are the "brains": each one of the Euclid computers is located at a different site, at Vélizy in the Paris region and at Toulouse. In computer-assisted production, three production centers — located in Signes, Salbris and Le Chesnay — are equipped with digitally controlled tool-machines, programmed by means of a Compact II system of simultaneous programming that accesses a network of shared time. At the end of 1983, Matra's military division announced plans for a permanent liaison between the CAI Euclid complex and the CAP production centers.

If we attempt to summarize the evolution of telematic modes of production and its drastic reduction of the conception–production cycles, we will find that the small sub-contractor still uses the traditional means while the large sub-contractors use recording tape. Then — at the far end of the scale, as with Matra — we find the network, including direct intercommunication among digital image, virtual memory, and the constructed piece by means of transfer machines. Soon these machines will replace the primary machines. This has extraordinary implications for the reorganization of management-operation trees, for the readjustment of work assignments, and for all industrial arrangements and architectures.

Even this picture is incomplete until we take into account the connected development, in aerospace for example, of a final interactive system, a "computer-assisted representation" system (CAR), such as the electronic Diaporama:

"With this system, in five minutes you receive the ATR 42 airplane program along with the different modes engaged (by aerospace and Aeritalia) for the construction of the equipment, the advertising, sales and after-sales services, including different typical cases for exploitation corresponding to the performance of the plane in different configurations. The airline companies can thus dialogue interactively with the CAR to study different seat and freight arrangements, for example. They can check the primary working principles, such as speed, altitude, weight, fuel consumption, time in the air, reserves, and so forth. These are all posted in real time on the screen as a function of the characteristics of forecast stages, such as the length of runway and landing strips, the distances between layovers, the possibilities of being diverted, and so on."[8]

This computer-assisted representation, which replaces static reports of aeronautic material, is actually a work tool that integrates the informers, the directors and the users into one interactive terminal.

This capacity to integrate the future of the finished product is also developed at the level of the project, by means of "computer-assisted dynamic information" (CADI). This system allows one to study, from its origins, the growth of cells, the deformation of structures, the cracking and erosion of surfaces, the diverse forms of decay of an object that does not yet exist, all the while without forgetting the typology of its foreseeable accidents.

The second example concerns vehicular architecture, specifically the configuration of the future supersonic fighter-plane with high maneuverability (HIMAT), in which the control of the lift has to be integrally assured by electronics. In this plane, the wings lose their use as support and lift in order to participate in the directiveness of the flight pattern, variable geometry having already outlined this form of high technology. The fundamentally unstable airplane has evolved to the high speeds of constant freefall, in terms of altitude and direction, and thus is established a kind of permanent re-equilibrium. Although this technique is still in its experimental stages, it already points to that future towards which electronics is already headed. With the HIMAT, electronics supports the vehicle to the same extent as the energetic power of its propeller. If the plane is kept aloft by the speed of ejection of its jetpipes, it is not because of its fixed wing surfaces. It stays in the air because a highly complex central power-station assures the balancing of the engine by means of receivers distributed across the surface of the plane. These interchangeable elements possess a flexibility that is controlled point-by-point, in a manner reminiscent of the dolphins' echolocation envelope.

Basically, instantaneous feedback of the facts of flight create the immaterial support for an apparatus that is for all intents and purposes deprived of sustaining surfaces. This programmed instability — this constantly differentiated accident of effective release — permits a hitherto unequalled maneuverability at the highest speeds ever. By linking the speed of ejection of the engine's jet-pipe to the speed of information of the central station of inertia, we can now attain a telematic control of lift that is completely liberated from the impediments of the traditional airplane cell. Flight is freed of wings, rudders, ailerons, flaps, tail fins, and all the other stabilizers.

While informatics is integrated with telematics, in the instantaneity of transmission over long distances, it is also, as in this case, integrated with a restricted object. The end of the great distances of time exhausts more than just geometric dimension and the geographical organization of industrial and urban territories. It also takes over the proportions and design of the engine. With measures of distance-speed, such as the machometer and the millisecond, the extension of the apparatus undergoes a pressure analogous to that felt by the territorial dimension. We could call this pressure dromospherical; the technical object undergoes a deformation that is inherent to the rapidity of transfer of information.

The speed of transmission of the facts of flight affects the form of the engine, just as the relative wind that arises from the air resistance to an advancing plane did before. We are now witnessing the merger of telematics and aerodynamics, to the point where we could call the plane *teledynamic,* instead of supersonic or hypersonic, since the speed of information is closer to that of light than that of sound.

Basically, where the televised form-image results from the rapidity of particles that are accelerated by the cathode tube, our perception of the plane is really only a *virtual image,* a hologram that emerges somewhat from the speed of aerodynamic wind, but more essentially from the excessive dynamic of informatics. This virtual image is the result of a mode of energetic formation that contributes to a transmutation of physical appearances.

⊛　⊛　⊛

"Form is the base that rises to the surface." This poetic definition of *interface* now extends beyond the aerodynamic mode of formation that emerges from the informational capacities of airplane electronics. The final configuration of equipment such as HIMAT results less from the external constraints of the atmosphere than from the internal constraints of the "dromosphere," or of the instantaneity of transfer of data among the receivers distributed all over the surface of the engine and the central inertial generator. Each one of these receivers — or punctum of informatic action — acts, by means of a central inertial generator, on the form of the vehicle and the configuration of its flight, very much like pixels in the configuration of the synthetic form-image on the computer screen.

The role played by computer screens and tracer tables in the elaboration of fractal geometry is analogous to that of the telescope and microscope in the perception of the infinitely large and the infinitesimally small. This technology permits Mandelbrot to see, beyond the graphs, a complex synthetic imagery and the projection of a fractionary landscape. This allows the visual verification of a perfectly abstract theory, which is what the mathematician meant when he said, "Very quickly, I became used to illustrating my ideas, before they had a chance to mature, because the illustration facilitated the maturation."[9] With this, we develop a better understanding of the nature of interface, its function as opto-electronic informatic source, replacing the fastidious mathematical verifications of the past.

When, in 1968, the acceleration of the calculation of certain numerical tables played a major role in laying the ground for Mandelbrot's work, the acceleration of projection of numerical images was to become itself a veritable scientific confirmation, to the extent that specialists concerned with the results of work in geometry "would no longer be able to distinguish between data and traces on the screen."[10] This must have encouraged Mandelbrot, who in 1975 wrote, "For someone who enjoys geometry, the best test, in the final analysis, will always rely on the judgment one's eye transmits to one's brain. For this kind of geometry, the computer, with its graphic software, is today an unsurpassable tool."[11]

Finally, the fractionary dimensions are the heirs to that Lost Dimension, the informatic punctum, the pixel that allows the instantaneous projection of data, the representation of a synthetic, digital form-image which — as we saw with the supersonic apparatus — is also a presentation in true size of a form-object, an interactive airplane cell whose most refined performances are those of Brownian motion or, more precisely, Brownian flight.

Keeping in mind the role of turbulence studies for both Richardson and Mandelbrot, and the importance of the analysis of Brownian motion for the elaboration of "fractals," we almost naturally compare the research of a greater aeronautic maneuverability — based on the control of incessant releases of direction and altitude — with the research of accidents, of fractals, in the continuous variation of entire dimensions. Richardson's studies of variations in coastal distances and Mandelbrot's studies of continuous variations of dimensions cannot be separated from a new perception of space. This relativist perception insists on no longer sublimating the equivalence of distances and speeds in the *representations of figures* as much as in the *configuration of objects*. With this perception, we end up thinking of dimensions as both *entropic* in the thermodynamic sense and *informatic,* in the way Claude Shannon describes that term in his information theory. This helps to clarify not only the crisis of "whole" dimensions but, specifically, the ways in which our habitual notions of surface, of limit and separation, have decayed, and given way to those of interface, commutation, intermittence and interruption. These changes have great impact on conception and construction, right on down to building technologies and techniques. By making visible figures that would be otherwise imperceptible, infography exterminates the three dimensions, just as holography exterminated relief and direct-broadcast television exterminated the depth of field of real space.

The opto-electronic terminal is for Mandelbrot what the optic telescope was for Galileo and what cinemacroscopy was for Jean Painlevé. Each of these technologies produced for their time a displacement of appearances. This transfer brought entities, substances and distinct elements into the light, but more importantly it produced an absolute trans-

110

parence, a transitivity in which the primary standard of whole dimensions had to be abandoned and forgotten in favor of the standard of transfer of fractionary dimensions. In this irruption, the geometric dimensions become, for the planners, nothing more than momentary surface effects, just as depths of geographic space are for travellers in a world of supersonic tourism, erasing not only the coastal distances of Brittany but also the whole of the Atlantic Ocean (given the last thirty years, in which trans-Atlantic travel has been cut from 24 hours down to three-and-a-half).

The framework for the planner's point of view in the computer screen now resembles neither that of spectators and telespectators, nor the frames of reference for graphic or photographic representation, precisely because the computer screen contains them all, united now into the same interface, one single commutation of vision that dispels all normative distinctions between the real and the simulated.

This is what Kandinsky meant when he said, "The laws of harmony that are internal today will be external tomorrow." Representation now stretches beyond the real.[12] It extends beyond perceptual appearances and traditional conceptual frameworks, so that we can no longer discern differences of nature among objects and figures. It seems that the advanced audiovisual and automotive technologies have denatured direct observation and common sense.

Cinematographic and videographic techniques — the artisanal invention of dissolves, feedback, slow-motion and time-lapse, zoom, live and delayed broadcast — now appear to have been premonitory signs, symptoms of a de-realization of sensory appearances. These technologies proposed a question that was elaborated most succinctly by Jean-Luc Godard: "It seems to me increasingly that the sole great problem of film, in each movie, is where and why to begin a shot and why complete it? … Basically, life fills the screen in the way that a faucet is filling a bathtub that is letting out exactly the same amount of water at the same rate."

This question is essential to movie directors and to policy makers, professionals, urbanists and architects. In the context of contemporary scientific indeterminism, the crisis of dimensions is also a symptom. Ours is a crisis of cutting and joining, a crisis of editing; we have passed beyond the crisis of montage.

This is a crisis of representation rather than construction; as such, it involves macroscopy as much as microscopy. For example, when the scanner and the positron camera registers the activity of air in and around the brain, we are offered what pretend to be mental images of the mind. With this technology, we begin to visualize an *imago* whose concrete character has already been confirmed by the neurobiologist Jean-Pierre Changeux: "The materiality of mental images can no longer be doubted."[13] He further refutes the distinction between object and image by entitling one of the chapters of his book "Mental Objects" — as if the virtual images of informatics as well as televisual images were only the syndrome of a coming transparence that would affect, this time, consciousness itself.

⊛   ⊛   ⊛

With these mental objects, scientific materialism falls into its own trap; it is forced to accord density to that which visibly has none: figures of the imaginary and virtualities of consciousness. Where before microscopes, telescopes and other means of improved observation allowed us to see that which we could not really see, the newer advanced technologies of investigation now have given body and corporeality to that which before had none.

After the discovery of the magnifying powers of optic lenses and Galileo's uses of the astronomical telescope, after E. J. Marey's invention of chronophotography and Painlevé's macro-cinematrographic use of the imperceptible, we now arrive at the emergence of the incorporeal. The figure becomes an object entire unto itself as the *imago* becomes an objective image. This happens when psychologists describe the *imago* in terms of space and dimensions. For example, Stephen M. Kosslyn has written: "Mental images appear in a sort of three-dimensional space. This in no way means that images occur in a real three-dimensional space, but rather in an environment that possesses certain functional properties in common with that type of space. For example, this is the case with a three-dimensional matrix in a computer's memory: it is three-dimensional space in a functional rather than a physical sense."[14]

We prefer to call it *matrix,* since the term *functional* leads too quickly to the delirium of interpretation that comes from confusing figure with object, an analogical conflict that runs the length of the history of scientific knowledge. This analogy is composed of surveying metaphors, whose reference basis is not only measurement and filming but also and equally the displacement of the object in its representation. After the geodesic measure of the Meridian arc by La Condamine and his colleagues; after Delambre and Mechain's measures at the dawning of meteorology; and, more recently, after Richardson and Mandelbrot's measurement of the coast of Britanny; we now have Kosslyn — professor of psychology at Harvard University — who in 1980 proposed to the subjects in his experiment: survey a mentally drawn island with the purpose of testing the equivalence between cartographic distances and the temporal distances of mental travel.

Kosslyn asked his subjects to design a map of an island with a beach, a shack, rocks, trees, and so forth, spread out at precise locations. Then, he removed the map and asked them to use "their imagination" and explore the beach, the shack, the trees. According to Kosslyn, the significant fact is that the time-span of the imaginary surveying varied in a linear manner with the real distances marked by the subject on the map, as if the mental cartography contained the same information about the distances as did the real map.

Since mental images attracted the attention of nineteenth-century psychologists; the invention of photography fit them to a tee. And if today we are witnessing a revival of this kind of scientific interest (to the great dismay of the behaviorists), the recent developments in infography and holography certainly make sense. Where once the *clichés* resulting from the exposure time of photographic plates brought a first semblance of explication, now the virtual images of the computer screen seem to confirm not only the existence of certain forms of representation but, more immediately, the objective presence of mental images. In neurobiology especially, these representations are losing their status as virtual images and becoming mental objects — as indicated by J. P. Changeux when he concluded, "It is not utopian to think that one day we will be able to see the image of a mental object appearing on a computer screen."

This new approach to visual thinking — contrary to that of Rudolph Arnheim[15] — is emerging from developments in photo-cinematography, and seems to relegate notions of exposure time and speed to a secondary level, elevating systems of traditional coordinates instead. We have already seen how the study of properties of mental image can do this only by displacements, rotations, and translations that require the examination of distances of time and the accounting of the speed of execution of imaginary motions. Practically reciting Shepard and Metzler's terms, Changeux describes the determination of forms as a sort of mental rotation in three-dimensional space, occurring with a speed of some 60 degrees per second. In Changeux's world, mental imagery finally acts as if it possessed both a physical rigidity and a measurable speed of rotation.

To commit oneself to this kind of recycling in order to

discuss mental space — to re-invoke the dimensional and matrix components as markers of physical and geophysical space — seems an absurdity, an analogical absurdity that tries to cut corners on the temporal characteristics of those representations. The reinsertion of the old baggage of the resolution of the geometric image into the examination of images of the absence of image is to voluntary forego those elements of interpretation essential to any understanding of the mode of formation of mental space: namely, photography, cinematography, and above all holography. From this scene of redundancy emerges a critical question. In which light do mental images appear? What day do they inhabit?

The problem of the form-image is not primarily one of geometrical formation.[16] The problem is one of modes of appearance and disappearance in the context of light. The context is that of the substance of light, solar, chemical, electrical or other. Contemporary physics has taught us to consider this substance as material. Optic and energetic technologies of photosensitivity have accustomed us to using light by means of the photographic plates of the past, film, photosensitive cells, radiography, and, most recently, the invention of *ideography*, allowing us to see the figurative action of cerebral air — the positron camera capable of detecting photons, or quanta of light, thanks to the multitude of photosensitive cells distributed around the cranium of the conscious subject.

We are cutting corners at the very instant in which the laboratory is prepared to pass from the electronic stage of the transistor to the photonic stage of the transphaser, or optic transistor. We are taking shortcuts as we stand on the brink of producing a veritable optic computer, using variations of intensity of pencils of light, instead of electrical currents, much like fibre-optic systems, and capable of performing thousands upon thousands of operations per second. These quick fixes and shortcuts deprive us of the bases for reasoning that are necessary for the examination of figurative properties of the imaginary, and equally for the philosophic and scientific redefinition of notions of space, time and dimension.

While we observe today the succession of form-images that offer themselves to our direct, indirect or delayed perception, we note that we are, once again, in the presence of a self-enclosed system, a system of representation the exact configuration of which no one is ready to estimate.

We have journeyed from the mental images of image and loci, to the ocular, binocular and optic image, and then from the graphic, photographic, cinematographic and videographic images through the holographic and infographic images, to the most recent — ideographic — image: that mental image, recuperated in the mirror of advanced technologies, that completes the operations of radioscopy and endoscopy, offering to us for contemplation not only our internal organs but our very thoughts. We stand now before a veritable kaleidoscope, a depot of images and figures whose coherence is never doubted, persuaded as we have been since the Quattrocento of the unity of the real and its representation.

Before long we will be forced to undergo a lacerating revision of our figurative conceptions. This "reconstruction" involves more than physicists and philosophers. It embraces architects, urbanists, and other geometricians, because the product of today's man / machine interface, the overexposure of screens, is also the product of the man / environment face-to-face encounter, the exposure of immediate vision. If, in the physics of the infinitesimally small, the appearance of surfaces hides a secret transparence that is a thickness without thickness and a volume without volume, then the greatest lengths of time and the widest expanses no longer occult direct vision. Today, the perception of facts has given way to unprecedented facts of perception. While these facts of perception can readjust the components of consciousness, no one can apprehend their sensate reality.

The Lost Dimension

In 1933 in the RCA laboratories, Vladimir Zworykin, the inventor of the iconoscope (as television was first called), was not dreaming of a means of mass information. He was seeking to broaden the scope of human view by perfecting the electric eye. He proposed to install his apparatus on a rocket to observe inaccessible regions of space —anticipating by some years the Pioneer, Voyager and Explorer missions. This helps to explain the equivalence between telescopic or tele-visual optics and energetics, an equivalence that now trembles on the brink of a fusion of the vectors of accelerated, electronic or photonic representation and those of hypersonic commu-nication, such as the airplane, missile, or satellite. In this fusion / confusion of the real and its representation, the analogy of the optic illusion and the motor illusion is con-firmed. The renowned "conquest of space" is shown to be nothing more than the acquisition of one image among many, a "form-image" that is definitively without any objectivity.

Under these conditions, the relativist equivalence of lengths and speeds become a "fact of perception," an immedi-ate *datum* of consciousness with the same status as Euclid's postulate. No longer sublimated, speed is now recognized as that which gives form to images — to images of conscious-ness, such as mental and ocular images, and to our con-sciousness of optic or opto-electronic images. If speed is now the shortest route between two points, the necessarily reduc-tive character of all scientific and sensible representation becomes a reality effect of acceleration, an optic effect of the speed of propagation. This speed is metabolic in the example of ocular and mental images, and technological in the case of the form-images of photographic and cinematographic repre-sentation, of the virtual images of infography, and of the representations of optic lasers.

We are presently engaged in a generally misunder-stood event that seems to offer comfort to this view. To the two Euclidean and non-Euclidean geometries are added, with all

117

apparent legitimacy, two spaces, two physical conceptions. On the one hand, we have the space of classical Newtonian mechanics, in which no interaction can occur between a field, such as an electric or electromagnetic field, and the void (since the classical void is by definition a state in which there is neither matter nor energy). On the other hand, according to quantum mechanics, even the void has a structuring principle that can modify the propagation of force fields.

According to the physician Claudio Rebbi, "The structure of the void is a consequence of Heisenberg's uncertainty principle. One version of this uncertainty principle declares that, for every physical event, there exists an uncertainty concerning the quantity of energy released during the event, and this uncertainty is directly related to the uncertainty about the exact moment in which the event occurred. Thus, for every event of extremely brief duration, there exists a great uncertainty about the energy. Hence, during every very short interval of time, there exists a strong probability that the quantum void possesses a non-null packet of energy."

The structure of the void, the energy of the void that is able to manifest itself through the spontaneous creation or annihilation of a particle, appearance or disappearance of a field in diverse regions of space: without prejudging the scientific validity of these propositions, we can at least intuit the importance of this notion of interaction after that of interface, both equally in the conceptions of theoretical physics and the advance of questions of communication and telecommunication, the appreciation of "tele-topological" phenomena. This has direct consequences in the matter of management of space and time, especially if we recall that every interactive system presumes confinement, inertia, and degrees of liberty. One day soon, this inertial confinement could easily take the place of the real displacement of people and objects, just as that displacement once took the place of metropolitan enclosure and sedentariness.

5
Critical Space

Given the interactive image and the interactive city, and if every image is destined for growth, in the epoch of non-separability this destiny is accomplished before our very eyes, thanks to the mutual development of the electronic urban environment and the architecture of systems, an improbable architecture whose efficiency none can deny.

Ubiquity, instantaneity, and the populating of time supplant the populating of space. The durable management of continents has given way to the generalized incontinence of transfers and transmissions. Along with the 300 million tourists per year and the 100,000 daily airline passengers, one must also count the hundreds of millions of auto commuters, waiting for their endless mobs of telematic speakers and tele-actors of transfer machines. From this swirl emerges the decay of grand political and juridical systems, through decolonization, decentralization and the first stages of post-industrial dis-urbanization.

Measuring the effects of these three phenomena in Europe and the United States, we remain silent about the phenomenon of hyper-concentration going on in certain megalopolises, such as Mexico City — that capital city that is devouring the nation, and which will boast 40 million inhabitants by the end of the century — or Shanghai or Sao Paulo, each already embracing some 30 million residents. But no urbanist worthy of that name could interpret this hyper-concentration as a sign of the survival or revitalization of urban living. We all see this hyper-concentration as a mass-critique: as a cataclysmic index of the quickly approaching disintegration of the historic town, of traditional urban development, and of the State.

Basically, the geopolitics of nations that until recently assumed the hierarchical privilege of center over periphery, of summit over basis, and of "radioconcentrism" of lateral exchanges and communications, has lost its value at the same instant that extreme vertical densification lost its power. Both gave way to an unapparent morphological configuration, in which the *nodal*[1] replaced the *central* in a preponderantly electronic environment, in which "tele-siting" favored the deployment of a generalized ex-centricity, an unbounded periphery. This advance notice of the end of the rule of industrial urban life also announced the end of metropolitan sedentariness. In its stead, we find an obligatory interactive confinement, a kind of inertia of human population, for which the term *teleconcentrism* might well be proposed, just as we wait for the word "homeland" to replace the idea of the great suburb.

With the notion of homelands, the secular opposition of town and country ceases, and at the same time that the geomorphological unity of the State dissolves. Gone is all autonomy understood as the conditional independence accorded to different local sub-sections. We now have instead an internal extraterritorial entity which, as it abolishes the niceties distinguishing metropolitan inhabitation from colonial population, does away with the rule of the city, the very necessity of political citizenship for the administered populations. This, of course, is already the case in the ten homelands in South Africa, which came into being between 1975 and 1976 through the devices of the Pretoria government. Eighty percent of the South African population lives beneath the poverty line, eight million Black Africans lost their South African citizenship in order to be made into citizens of a second zone of "independent" concentration States. Under autocratic control and baptized as "City-States" or "Nation-States," they are completely deprived of agricultural and industrial resources. Sometimes, as with the Kwandebele, they have no access to water. They all depend exclusively on the money sent back by immigrant workers.

As the perfect accomplishment of the colonial system, and the re-ascendence of forms of subjugation rightly rejected over twenty years ago, South Africa's Grand Apartheid — as well as the separatist regimes systematically developed in Asia, the Middle East and elsewhere — are not the abrogation of the previously described principle of non-separability. They are its confirmation, for these discriminatory practices mark the advent of a post-industrial *endo-colonialism* that supplanted the earlier exo-colonialism of central Empires in the industrial age. This inversion results, on the one hand, from the de-industrialization of metropolitan agglomerations, from the progress of automation, and from the decline of the work force, and, on the other hand, from the instantaneous, interactive functions of technology that privilege multinational monopolistic intensitivity at the expense of national capital extensivity.

What's here today is tendentiously disqualified by what's beyond the horizon. If that which is present is potentially discredited by the immediacy of that which is absent or deferred, then the metropolitan concentration no longer makes sense. Urban agglomeration has lost its reason for being, just as happened with the now-defunct colonial Empires. Then the national State disappears in the moment of replication, just as the city-state proliferated just prior to disappearing in favor of the single capital, the political pole of the nation-state formation.

Since what is interactive is also interchangeable, the urban has lost its form, with the sole exception of the form-image without dimension, the point or punctum which is everywhere while the measurable length is nowhere. In the manner of the nodal and the Pascalian node, this center which rejects all circumference and even the very concept of periphery is the uncertainty principle applied to the world geomorphological continuum. As such, it prolongs the geometric abstraction of the ancient City as the inventive *polis* of a political isonomy and of the State of rights for its resident citizens, native or assimilated. The decline of this State of civil law is as evident today as is that of the metropolis. The deterioration of the notion of the "rights of man" clearly indicates the current crisis. The crisis of national identity becomes the crises of territorial citizenship and local authority. Together, these create a kind of crisis of excess that affects places, people, justice, and law.

This political crisis is comparable to the crisis in the notion of dimension. As the advent of a sort of trans-political disinformation — actually an excess of information — it is curiously analogous to the fractionary character of our recent conceptions of matter in physical theory. Our present uncertainty as regards the status of people and places comes from the historical evolution of law, beginning with the first land-taxes at the agrarian and pre-geometric origins of society, passing through the vicissitudes of maritime law, as with the International Conference of Ocean Rights, and law of the skies, as with airline deregulation, and ending at the present spatial, sidereal law. With this history, we arrive at a perspective without horizon or, better, a perspective whose horizon is negative, in the sense of that dark film destined to make an impression on our retina.

This new horizon is constructed of momentary law, legislation of instantaneity, tribunals of exception, government by decrees and ordinances, and a state of urgency. These are indices of a transpolitical intensitivity that destroys the permanence of laws, the long duration of legally based rights, the persistance of a civil State. That persistence is vitiated by instability in employment and housing and by constant "trans-border" exchanges and floods. Everywhere we look, we find signs of the decrepitude of a civil peace whose most advanced technologies incessantly threaten to destroy accomplishments, and for which the notions of State terrorism and aggression already indicate the probable outcome.

In the dis-urbanization of Cambodia by the Khmer Rouge and the realization of Grand Apartheid in South Africa, we find the creation of internal extraterritorial precipitates, homelands for indigenous populations reduced to the level of untouchables. At the same time, we cannot forget that part of metropolitan deregulation caused by the disindustrialization of the European and American agglomerations, the devastation of the grand urban centers such as Detroit, Chicago, Cleveland, and St. Louis, cities now discredited as centers of American industrial regions. Entire cities, now ruined, suffer the fate their own inner-city neighborhoods underwent when they were transformed into ghettoes for persecuted and oppressed populations.

These cities appear to be the inverse of those of South Africa, where the suburbs are the White Zones, but they are in fact identical. This helps to explain recent elections of Black mayors and the arrival of urban Black majorities. The transformation of the major cities of the Eastern seacoast of the United States into crime zones and slum cities is identical to the urban history of England during the Depression. This helps explain President Reagan's plans as regards "civil defense," as demonstrated in 1982 by his approval of a seven-year plan to relocate two-thirds of the United States population, slotting over four million dollars for the project. Thus, during the 1980's, some 380 high-risk regions were to be evacuated into as many regions of provisional relocation, thereby doubling the percentage of survivors hoped for in case of a nuclear conflict.

Behind this program for metropolitan redeployment, we can divine the real thoughts of those in charge of the State of the Union. Economic deregulation — the favored position of American new economists — would therein reach its climax. The monetary and tariff "grand disorder" roughly proposed by multinationals at the beginning of the 1970s could now become the rule of urban management. The pauperization of the Andean sub-continent would reach the whole of the American continent.

By abandoning those populations that had become superfluous and unproductive, thanks to the advances of automation and the progress of tele-informatics, the crepuscular end of the providence-State would find a voluntary geography characterized by the bankrupting of all public assistance: the geopolitics of urgency, unemployment and destitution. Out of this would emerge the post-industrial and transpolitical destiny-State founded on threat, on apocalyptic risk as opposed to political enemies, the economic rival, the social adversary or partner. This would turn the tables on all History, for it would mean the end of the principles of territorial assembly and of the law of the city, and in which places, people and things became interchangeable at will.

From this angle, decentralization assumes, especially in France, a meaning altogether different from that of regional autonomy. It comes to mean the end of the unity of place of the old political theater of the City and its imminent replacement by a unity of time, a chronopolitics of intensitivity and interactivity. In this, technics replace the long duration of the City, as systems architecture definitively replaces the contemporary system of architecture and urbanism.

⊛　⊛　⊛

Alternative or marginal ideologies are not civil resistance to oppression. Instead, in the manner of liberation ideologies, they anticipate situations of abandonment that are actively sought after by the powers of extraordinarily diverse communities in attendance. These include international and national communities as well as social and family partners, working together irrespective of their economic situations or their political regimes.

Calls for worker management and worker control — posted by unions — correspond to and are echoed by the call for a minimum State — broadcast by the new economists. Their argument relies on the productive capacities of technologies that reduce the need for full employment, and thus the real and effective presence of workers.

The demand for autonomy is a symptom of a collective and simultaneous desire for inertia. It is the inertia that characterizes the non-separability of current events and their confinement, whose uncontrolled amplitude has already been demonstrated by the rising ecology movements. For example, North American survivalists offer the hope of "free spaces" for the marginal and the counter-culture and, at the same time, the making of an acculturation that serves the working goals of American neo-conservatism.

To the extent that their references, — atomic apocalypse, recession, pollution — are identical, the survivalist movement is inscribed into the same eschatological perspective as the ecology movement. Guided by rejection of the modern city and opposition to economic dependence and public assistance, founded on the urgent necessity of a metropolitan diaspora, survivalism (with its four million adherents) re-enforces the tendency towards the emancipation of populations and confirms the premature termination of the town / country attraction. This last has already been indicated by industrial and financial redeployment patterns, and by Civil Defense measures recently taken by the U.S. territorial administration. These all point to an organized regression that will entail the advent of a post-industrial politics of self-subsistence to accompany self-defense policies, with all that suggests for the decomposition of societies, of life styles and of customary urbanity.[2]

One issue seems decisive in the question of territorial and social organization. Instead of opposing an adversary or a declared enemy, we respond to a menace, or supposed danger, with economic, ecological and strategic plans, plans which in no way promise a later re-assembly or a geographic or demographic regrouping. We have instead pro-active dismemberment, the redeployment of threatened units of production, habitation or administration. We dimly see a centrifugal and socially deterrent process that today contributes — through the organization of territorial populations — to the rending of the social and familial tissue that was inherited from a recent past of productivity. This productivity emerged from a workforce that was necessarily abundant and massive, comprised, as it was, of both industrial labor and conventional armed forces. The decay of the armed forces has been under-estimated as regards the meaning of the draft and of military service. The decline of the armed forces is in every instance comparable to the decline of employment that itself prefaces the decline of citizenship by law.

After the explosion of the ancient extended family that arose from rural living, the present disintegration of the urban nuclear family progressively relieves threatened populations of any prospect for organized resistance. The call for the autonomy of women and children, the autarchy often sought for by unemployed or fugitive fathers, the forced separation of parents and grandparents, the high mobility and extreme precariousness of work, and the ultra-high frequency of household moves, all contribute to the withdrawal of the "primary weapon" from various collectivities, that basic cell of resistance to oppression that the family ultimately constitutes.

There is no more real civil concentration and almost no more valid political concentation. According to the new strategy, armaments involve neither the soldier nor the means employed. Armaments are about position, disposition, and direction of forces facing each other. Current metropolitan redeployment tends to definitively disarm the conjunctive systems of civil society, including the neighborhood and the family cell, on down to the very possibility of any opposition to oppression. In this day and age, oppression wears the uniforms of tyrannies other than those of a party, class or individual, since now the totalitarian unity proceeds disguised by the advances of civil and military technologies, advances that have no interest whatsoever in democracy.

If we consider the recent histories of popular opposition and of organized civil resistance, we see that the newest innovations are neither the riot nor the urban insurrection but rather the strike and especially the general strike, that inertia programmed in advance, propagated by the workers' syndicalists of the last century.

No longer a struggle for space, now time is interrupted. The ramparts, barricades, and the state of siege of an era of generalized extensivity have been replaced by work stoppages, occupations, and trade disruptions that signify an era of intense interactivity and a state of urgency that has become the routine. Unfortunately, this kind of revolutionary resistance works only in periods of full employment and growth. But in recessions — with their systematic abandonment of unskilled labor and deindustrialization — it is the employers' lock-out that becomes the rule, reversing all power dynamics.

"Technical" unemployment, "temporary" or "interim" employment, job-sharing, wage-sharing, all divisions of labor that contribute to the formation of workers' split personalities reverse the conditions and possibilities of any civil defensive, except perhaps for a general tax strike. Civil opposition to oppression and injustice no longer follows the path of armed struggle. Outside of the use of erratic weapons which it distributes freely, civil resistance now relies on the space-time of its daily processes. It uses its own milieu, the restrained morphological continuum which is its own. Thus, it is precisely the spatio-temporal apparatus that is devastated by the extraordinary flights of high technologies, and equally by the post-industrial redeployment resulting from the intense interactivity of "transborder" exchanges.

Terrorism is just one proof among many of the failure of democratic opposition, because it always involves a double reinforcement of coercion. The development of "forces of order" — the growing sophistication of their means of prevention, of their military hardware, and the probable erection of a police State within the democracies — followed by a period of armed struggle, result in the reactionary militarization of the best elements of the organized resistance, as has happened with the ETA and the IRA.

The obvious usefulness of armed popular struggle in wars of national liberation has deceived us about the operational value of guerrilla warfare, and the "decolonization" campaigns have actually served as propaganda for a particular kind of combat that has nothing in common with actual organized civil resistance.

Beyond the "guerrilla," the development of "terrorism" has made abundantly clear that — as the exotic form of a transpolitical delinquency and as the avatars of a desperate and dispirited minority — terrorism today offers no practical usefulness. If for André Malraux in 1930 the revolution was "a truck, some men and rifles," forty years later, for the Red Brigades, it has become a motorcycle, two men and a revolver. Following the logic of these logistics, by the end of the century all rebellion will be passive and inert, thanks to the force of things supporting the partisans of nonviolent civil disobedience.

Basically, the struggle for independence and the creation of new nation-States of the sort produced by various "liberation fronts" in the developing world has nothing in common with the resistance to metropolitan *endo-colonization* that we have attempted to consider. Finally, the generous illusion that characterized the epoch of the decline of long-distance coercion, the *exo-colonization* of the central Empires, also reached to the true nature of resistance to the era of technologies of proximal coercion.

The supposed ethics and politics of resistance to injustice are then vitiated by the absence of any analysis of the military question. Specifically, there has been no analysis of the extraordinary revolution in the mode of long-distance control and destruction — a revolution whose historical importance is equal to that of the revolution in modes of production in the last century, but whose consequences for civil society and for democracy have not yet been fully acknowledged or evaluated. The latest doctrines in matters of nuclear exchange allow the critical state to devise strategies of mutual deterrence which affect not only the redeployment of cities and businesses, but also that of missiles.

With recent advances in ballistics, everything happens in extremely short time-lapses: a few minutes is long-term, a few seconds or fractions of seconds is short-term. For example, the first-strike doctrine requires that, in order to reach their targets, nuclear missiles have to be discharged before the enemy's can be launched. Reaction time is so short that, in a period of international tension, peace or war are

129

decided by a computer network, the *launch on alert* system.

It is symmetrically the same when it comes to retaliation, as General Gallois, one of the primary spokespersons for the French retaliatory strike force, explained: "Retaliatory forces have to be on quasi-automatic pilot. This quasi-fatality of reaction to any threat is indispensable."

The critical State, or, better, the *Critical Space* described earlier, becomes critical by virtue of the instantaneity of means of mass *communication* as much as through the performances of delivery vectors of massive *destruction*. This is exactly what former U.S. Under-Secretary of Defense W.J. Perry meant when he explained, "If I wanted to sum up in a phrase the present discussion concerning precision missiles and saturation weapons, I would say that as soon as you can see the target, you can expect to destroy it."

The function of the eye becomes simultaneously that of the arm. The ancient astronomer's glass and Galileo's telescope are replaced by the telescoping of a nearly instantaneously inflicted destruction, and this irrespective of the distance or even the focal length.

The means of communicating destruction now join with those of information. The instantaneity of the televised interface becomes that of the viewing itself. Non-separability of military events in the firing mechanism of retaliatory operations underpins deterrence. From this reality emerges the character of the extreme urgency in all discussions about the crisis of nuclear deterrence, the seeming inevitability of a limited atomic war, and the idea of pre-emptive attacks. These discussions do not result from some will-to-power of the military giants of the East or West, but rather from the extreme rapidity of the means of detection and destruction of the third generation of weaponry. The extraordinary speed today tends to destroy all time for reflection, and thereby raises the question of how much time is necessary before any declaration of war. In so doing, the swiftness has erased the distinction between offensive and defensive, direct and indirect, and between the rear-guard and the vanguard of any retaliatory strike force, categories which once formed the basis for our strategy of deterrence, the balance of terror.

For example, John J. Maresca, legal counsel to the United States embassy in Paris, wrote: "In modern warfare the events will probably happen with as much rapidity as violence," and, "New dimensions (such as air space and withdrawn territories) will be added to those of the front lines on which the combatants engaged in traditional conflicts. As a result, in order to win, it makes sense now to pass immediately from the defensive to the pre-emptive attack on the rear-flanks of the enemy, as well as on the front line." In his own manner, Maresca reiterates the non-separability of exchanges in nuclear warfare, the fact that there, as elsewhere, "limitation" has become "commutation," the interchangeability of actions and positions.

Frome here on, the swiftness of exterminating engines is sanctioned in its own right: as the very essence of war, of that "pure war" that is capable of melting down the basic difference between defense and offense, a difference that used to mark both the conflict of wills between adversaries as well as the distinction between imposed war and preventive war. This fusion and confusion of situations, this reversibility of positions contributes, sooner or later, to the establishment, beyond the balance of terror, of State-against-State terrorism, which will involve the launching of preventive hostilities, as well as the launching of State-sponsored criminal campaigns, with incalculable consequences.

Ⓐ   Ⓐ   Ⓐ

In this interactive environment, the absence of extension is equivalent to the absence of delays. Time is so short between the first and second strike that it virtually abolishes any difference between unexpected attack and massive re-prisals, so that the point now is to keep the war-game partner–adversaries from firing the first shot.

The *right to pre-emptive strike* presently claimed by the Pentagon negates the depth of field of the adversary's territory and, even more disquietingly, denies the depth of time required for any kind of reasonable response, which is after all the basis for credibility for atomic peace between East and West. From here emerges the desire to prepare public opinion, especially in Europe, for the eventuality of a nuclear war — a "tactical" atomic war which the American forces pretend they can win by means of "early offensive operations." *Pre-emptive strikes* is just another name for the preventive war that will result not so much from the will-to-power of American or Soviet superpowers as from the power of new war materiel itself, the power of instantaneous deliv-ery that someday soon will transform war into involuntary response, definitively shattering the world's fragile balance.

In effect, the defensive became "offensive" when stra-tegic deterrence served primarily to intensify the arms race in "tactical" weapons, with incessant scientific and technical improvements in the vectors of conventional and nuclear delivery systems, acceleration of speed, multiplication of explosive charges, and refined precision in guidance systems. From that point on, every place became the front line, exposed in advance to instantaneous destruction. *Everything is overexposed in the interface of an interactivity that strips reality of the possibility of places, things, or adversaries meeting face to face.* Simultaneously, this development erases all military notions and all political and geopolitical concepts that essentially resulted from that *unity of time and place* that has vanished before our very eyes.

For more than a decade, this progressive de-realization of relationships of force between the East and the West has affected strategic reasoning in terms of the doctrine of use of war materiel, creating a mounting confusion between the "doctrine of production" (industrial logistics) and the "doctrine of use" (basic military strategy). If we are not careful, we will proceed to a political decision about warfare that will result in the fatal construction of the *automation of the declaration of war,* the transpolitical invention of a "machine for the declaration of war," the engine of the Final Judgment, the Domesday Machine that will complete the innovation of war machines that began with the birth of historical time.

Already, the foreseeable consequence of Euromissile deployment has led some experts to seriously envision the construction in 1984 of *automated deterrence.* According to Egon Bahr, for example, "We anticipate the Soviet Union deploying SS-22 missiles with 900 kilometer range and SS-23 missles with 500 kilometer range in both Czechoslovakia and East Germany. This will create a new situation in which Soviet missiles will be able to reach their objectives anywhere in West Germany in under two-and-a-half minutes. We will be faced with a system of automatic firing."

While this threat is overwhelming at the level of local exchanges, it also signals the end of responsibility of heads of State in the declaration of hostilities, along with the definitive submission of political and diplomatic intelligence to the military. We are forced to admit that the quasi-fatality of the use of retaliatory strikes, first predicted by General Gallois, leads now to the elimination of any human intervention in the cycle: *detection, designation, pursuit and engagement of weapons.* We have been abandoned to the care of a cybernetic procedure, with all the repercussions that implies for East–West relationships.

Extending Eisenhower's last address, of 1961, in which he attacked the military–industrial complex, President Carter, in his farewell address, stated, "It may be only a matter of time before the madness, the hopelessness, the covetousness or the errors in evaluation releases this terrifying force. A global nuclear war will release a destructive power superior to that unleashed in the entirety of the Second World War, and this, *in each second* of that long afternoon that will be necessary for the launching of all the missiles and the unloading of all the bombs. *Each second will experience the Second World War,* and the first few hours will tally more deaths than were involved in all the wars of History combined."

It is a matter of time, effectively, in which we can ask: Which would be more terrifying, the quantity of destruction and mortality inflicted, or the extreme rapidity of events that will overtake us with the devastating power of its swiftness? This total One-Second War is a war of time that results in the non-separability of events, and it is comparable to the frontal telescoping of two vehicles that, upon reaching certain high velocities, are replicated instead of diminished. In this *mirror effect* of the speed of propagation of messages and of missiles, the direct responsibility of the human decider, the head of State or the Chief of Staff, is erased, a fatal consequence of an arms race that was finally nothing more than the arming of the race towards inertia, a logistical confinement in which adversarial forces are mutually re-enforced at their own expense. All notions of parity and balance, the basis for mutual nuclear deterrence, have given way to multiplication effects that no one controls.

These induced effects come from the rapidity rather than the quantity of destruction of war materiel. Swiftness and acceleration of exchanges and communication have attained a critical threshold *in assuring the immediate reversibility of all actions and decisions.* We now face interactions in which adversaries instantaneously exchange their intentions and their offensive or defensive stances, to the point of confusing their ground position, their reciprocal convictions, and their sense of what will happen.

This situation no longer answers to the classical geostrategic scheme, which assumed the complementarity of offensive and defensive actions in each instant of armed engagement. The recent displacement by the "strategy of global intervention" of atmospheric, hydrospheric and lithospheric *space-time* to dromospheric and sidereal *space-speed* allows us to penetrate to an outer world that has no relationship to the world of military history. This outer world — or, better, "outer space" — could be mistaken for that of quantum mechanics, for that of the quantum of action, a form-image stripped of reality but somehow capable of abolishing classical physics (especially Newtonian space-time), and with it strategic and tactical reference systems that assumed a before-and-after, a present-past-and-future. In the classical system of time and space, protaganists still had identities, distinct wills and positions, general dispositions and directions of force.

Today, will and identity are mashed and blurred into the fusion / confusion of space-speed, in which characters and reciprocal characteristics are exchanged and swapped, forming a field of confrontation in which extent and depth, contrary to appearances, have less to do with atmospheric space than with the single "depth of time" of technical vectors, those vectors of infinite acceleration that have displaced war from its natural and human physical environment to its microphysical — instead of metaphysical — essence. This translation has happened not only at the level of the nuclear explosive device but — more importantly, and as of yet unnoticed — at the level of vectors of instantaneous delivery: intensified radiation weapons, directed-cluster missiles, laser cannons, implosive devices capable of destroying people and materiel and above all else the *field of combat*. Only yesterday that depth of field of nuclear warfare allowed us to distinguish, with our adversary, the stages of escalation: from the restrained conventional engagement to the generalized atomic war, passing through the possibility of a "limited nuclear war." This situation is now as grave as it can get, given the extent to which it eludes the grasp of civil and military personnel.

The will-to-power of those industrial nations who, at the turn of the century, practiced the techniques of total war, has now been replaced by the theoretical operation of a totally involuntary war, on the part of post-industrial nations investing increasingly in informatics, automation, and cybernetics. In these societies, the use of human labor-force and the direct responsibility of people has been displaced by the powers of "anticipated" and "deferred" substitution, the power of the system of auto-directed armaments, self-programmed detection networks, and automotic respondents who lead humanity to the confinement of a hopeless waiting.

The association of adversaries in the strategy of deterrence has turned into their sudden confusion, in the mixing and interface resulting from the dromospheric pressure of engines, delivery vectors moving at the speed of light, laser weapons, proton cannons, armaments using the energy of fusion. Remember that the dromospheric sphere, space-speed, is physically described by what is called the "logistic equation," the result of the product of the mass displaced by the speed of its displacement, $M \times V$. Since we have proceeded from important mass, such as the shell, the rocket, the missile, to elementary particles, the space of action is no longer that of dimensions, the space of classical physics. We now work the space of quantum mechanics, that of a "field" susceptible to fluctuation and to polarization in which the quantum of action is the unity of measure: a "unity" that occurs in neither extension nor duration, such that Einstein finally could exclaim: "We must stop describing atomic events as happening in space and time."[3]

Among these events we must now include atomic warfare, as a catastrophic probability that refers, not so much to the power of figures of State, as to the uncertainty principle in quantum physics. That principle prohibits the reconstitution of the trajectory of particles, by simple virtue of the fact that the trajectory does not exist! In the case of the radiation weapons that replaced ballistic instruments, the trajectory no longer exists. (As illustration, remember that the cathode tube responsible for the televisual interface is really an accelerator of particles, an electron cannon.)

President Reagan's warnings to the Soviet Union in March 1983 concerned the foreseeable deployment of multiple warhead missiles, using electromagnetic or corpuscular radiation: proton cannons, relative-electron cannons, weapons using properties of energy from thermonuclear fusion. In order to estimate the changes affecting the field of warfare, compare the target-site and the ballistic projectiles of the first and second generations of atomic weapons (the bomb, the shell, the rocket) to the cathode tube *screen,* the vacuum tube analogous to that of the third-generation armaments, which do not operate on the classic continuum. This generation is propelled in an enigmatic milieu in which *the container is no longer independent of the contents.* These weapons move through an ether recovered beyond classical physics, a quantum ether in which, like elementary particles, crowds and their directors bounce and flutter, obeying the same laws of probability, laws that have nothing to do with geopolitics or identity. In this world, the specificity of adversaries meeting face-to-face is first erased, and then disappears altogether, in favor of probable tendencies that no one controls. In the world of probabilities, scenarios, polls and other statistical manipulations refute the existence and value of the counsels of traditional diplomacy.

The same is true of the strategy of the East–West blocs. The absence of a field determines less the deployment of missiles in Europe or in the United States — be they SS-20s, Pershing 2s or MX missiles — than that of deterrent automatisms, the establishment of *automated decision-*

making in the matter of declarations of war. With the conclusion of the secular duel that once distinguished action from reaction and will to power from impotence, we have also lost the distinction between site and situation. We now have a *topology of the non-place* as a consequence of the non-sense of nuclear strategy, an "electronic" as much as an "atomic" war-game, in which the instantaneous interface replaces the face-to-face encounters of armies.

Instead of the grand battles of the past, we now have the darkroom mixing of an unprecedented violence in which the protagonists melt into each other, in the manner of their weapons, losing their singularity and with it their political will. The will-to-defense and the will-to-power are indifferently blended into a single amalgam. The definitive loss of the operational character of the means of destruction results in the too-great celerity of their long-distance delivery systems. The speed of violence becomes the violence of an unsurpassed speed, and the speed of light becomes the standard measure for war, for its context, its essence and its nature. *Pure war* contributes to the inversion of all terms of power, as it leads each antagonist to the immediate reversibility of the conditions of the possibility of confrontation.

We are observing the same movement as that which followed the primary discovery of gun powder, the invention and development of molecular explosives in Asia, the exploding pot and the use of pyrotechnic artifices. Then, in the West, with the invention of the cannon, shot, and shell, came the *management of the space-time of propulsion, the long-range projection of destruction,* which involved the augmentation of the initial speed of projectiles and of fire power, along with the concurrent scientific invention of ballistics. While ballistics was obviously essential to the development of shooting practices and fire plans, it was also necessary for the organization of both the City and the entire territory in the wake of feudalism and the emergence of monarchic centralism, the appearance of an absolute power, and the inertia of a national capital.

With nuclear explosives, everything begins again with a static weapon: the giant and immovable *bomb* in the New Mexico desert in 1945, and then with "Little Boy," the atomic bomb airlifted to Hiroshima. The race for power was also a race for smallness and lightness; it was this tri-partite aspect of the race that guided the first-generation weapons from nuclear fission to thermonuclear fusion and then, working on the shell, onto the development of atomic artillery.

Finally, after the race for the devastating power of the atom and the miniaturization of the charges of the second generation, we are now witnessing the launching of a race for speed and for precision of delivery. With extraordinary advances in electromagnetic and corpuscular "ballistics," warfare is propelled beyond classical space. With laser weapons, and with projectile weapons with warheads of neutral and charged particles (positive protons, neutrons or negative electrons), the third-generation armaments move beyond merely managing the space-time of deterrence (we still recall the episode with the red phone, the hotline) and organizing the intercontinental propulsion of destruction. The new generation also suppresses duration, extension and the depth of the geostrategic field by means of the instantaneity of an implosion in which the very free will of the antagonists is lost forever.

This extreme situation conditions the future of the City, the evolution of human populations, and the development and nature of all societies. If the invention of different war materiel contributed in the course of History to the definition of the urban form as a geopolitical arrangement, then the recent innovation of the *war immateriel* will soon contribute to the disarranging of the metropolitan agglomeration. Herein lies the significance of Reagan's "Seven Year Plan," not as a measure of effective civil defense but as a premonition of a future readjustment of the North American city into an information-tree for managing the defense of the United States. Sooner or later, this reorganization will lead to the re-examination of the urban concentration of the industrial age and to a new deranging, *the morphological irruption of the State of the Union,* a characteristic of the decay of territorial strategies and the advent of a "global logistics," the result of an intense telluric contraction of technics that leave post-modern societies with a solitary time arrangement. These societies arrive at the confinement of a last "capital," *the capital of dead time*, the inertial moment of a technical environment that has supplanted the sedentariness of the City, during that long span of geographic population in which the intensivity of communications and telecommunications replaced territorial extensivity. Then, the form-image of a population of time in which instantaneous transport and transmission will finally overcome the fixity of populations in the metropolitan space.

Finally, the grand movements of scientific and technical knowledge, the perception of an intimate state of matter, will have been only a series of procedures signalling in advance what was to follow at the heart of Occidental culture: the decay of visible markers, the loss of sensible referents, the disintegration of various "standards," excesses affecting the interpretation of phenomena and acculturation successively reaching to physics and geophysics, in order to pursue the astrophysical and cosmogenic quest for "the first moments of the universe," a retrospective inquiry that consists of climbing back through time with the aid of scientific certainties, in order to pose yet again the question of beginnings, the famous Big Bang, the explosion of causality that, according to physicists, was supposed to end tomorrow in a gigantic implosion of finality, a theoretical or meta-theoretical construction capable of saving the matter of the absence of sense, of preserving the creation of a creator, a secret desire for autonomy and for *universal automation* uniting all contem-

porary apocalyptic trends, this revelation of the precariousness of the human will, this face of hopelessness that is
perfectly matched to the degree of ambition among the
sciences, this deception in which the idea of nature from the
Enlightenment blurs into — and finally becomes confused
with — the idea of the real, left over from the century of the
speed of light.

June 1983

Notes

2
The Morphological Irruption

[1] Fernand Veger, "Le satellite et l'informatique au service du géographe," *Le Monde,* January 12, 1982.

[2] Dénis Randet, "Les écrans plat," *La Recherche,* #125, 1981.

[3] *Ibid.*

[4] Gaston Bachelard, *L'Intuition de l'instant,* Gallimard.

[5] Patrick Bouchareine, "Le mètre, la seconde et la vitesse de la lumière," *La Recherche,* #91, 1978.

[6] Florence Trystram, *Le Procès des étoiles,* Seghers, 1979.

[7] Bouchareine, *op cit.*

[8] Evry Schatzman, "La cosmologie: physique nouvelle ou classique?", *La Recherche,* #91, 1978.

[9] *Ibid.*

[10] *Ibid.*

[11] Paul Virilio, "L'engin exterminateur," *Silex,* #10, 1978.

[12] Louis de Broglie, *Continu et discontinue en physique moderne,* Albin Michel, 1941.

[13] This involved three experiments conducted at the Optics Institute at Orsay by Aspect, Dalibard, Grangier and Roger.

[14] Jean Petito, "Géometrie du hasard," *Traverses*, #24, 1982.

[15] Edmond Couchot, "Rhetorique de la technologie," *Traverses*, #26.

[16] Michel de Certeau:, "Rhetorique de la technologie," *Traverses*, #26.

[17] B. Mandelbrot, *Les Objets Fractals*, Flammarion, 1975.

[18] *Ibid.*

[19] In 1971, during the Apollo flight which allowed Armstrong to step onto the surface of the moon, I participated in a stunning phenomenon. Around two o'clock in the morning, while watching the first landing of a human on the moon, I saw the stars of the night, at the same time on my television screen and through my window. See my examination of this moment in "Le littoral vertical," in my book, *L'insécurité du territoire*, Stock, 1975.

[20] Among twentieth-century transcendental mathematics, logistics is far and away the most introspective. It involves a notation that allows for the enunciation and treatment of various propositions, all the while putting into relief continuities and discontinuities.

[21] *Theoria*, procession, parade, *processus*.

[22] Kurt Gödel, Princeton. Symbolic logic produced an important and yet curious theorem. Gödel's proof is a method that proves the existence of an object without ever producing the object.

[23] Paul Virilio, "La Dromoscopie ou la lumière de la vitesse," *Critiques*, 1978.

3
Improbable Architecture

[1] Walter Benjamin, *L'homme, le langage et la culture*, Denöel, 1971.

[2] *Ibid.*

[3] *Ibid.*

[4] "Film is the truth 24 times per second," Jean-Luc Godard.

[5] The Apple "Lisa" computer foregoes a keyboard in favor of a simple "electronic mouse" which is placed on a table, thereby likewise displacing the cursor on the screen.

[6] Benjamin, *op cit.*

[7] Marcel Pagnol, *Confidences,* Julliard, 1981.

[8] Paul Virilio, *Esthétique de la disparition,* Balland, 1980; *The Aesthetics of Disappearance,* trans. Philip Beitchman, Semiotext(e), 1991.

[9] In February, 1983, Chirac announced that Paris would have full cable access by 1989.

[10] Paul of Tarsus.

[11] By 1985, two Hughes satellites would assure telecommunications among the cities and the most remote recesses of Brazil.

[12] J. Abele and P. Malvaux, *Vitesse et univers relativiste,* Sedes, 1954.

[13] A. Einstein and L. Infeld, *L'évolution des ideés en physique,* Payot, 1974.

4
The Lost Dimension

[1] Paul Virilio, *Esthétique de la disparition,* Balland, 1980.

[2] G. Costa de Beauregard, *Le Second Principe de la science du temps,* Editions du Seuil, 1963.

[3] I. Prigogine and I. Stengers, *La Nouvelle Alliance,* Gallimard, 1979.

[4] B. Mandelbrot, *The Fractal Geometry of Nature,* Freeman and Co., 1982.

[5] William of Ockham, "One should not multiply the entities beyond the necessary," cited by Mandelbrot in *Débats,* March 1983.

[6] Aristotle, "There is no science of accidence."

[7] Octavio Paz, *Conjonctions et disjonctions,* Gallimard, 1971.

[8] Report of the CAO / FAO exhibit 83, given January 24, 1983, Paris.

[9] B. Mandelbrot, *Débats,* March 1983.

[10] *Ibid.*

[11] B. Mandelbrot, *Les Objets fractals,* Flammarion, 1975.

[12] B. d'Espagnat, *A la recherche du reél,* Gauthier-Villars, 1980.

[13] J.-P. Changeux, *L'Homme neuronal,* Fayard, 1983.

[14] Stephen M. Kosslyn, "Les images mentales," *La Recherche,* #108, 1980.

[15] Rudolph Arnheim, *La Penseé visuelle,* Flammarion, 1976.

[16] Edmund Husserl, *L'origine de la géometrie,* PUF, 1962.

5
Critical Space

[1] Nodal: a node of telecommunication and a pole of teledistribution.

[2] Accordingly, the municipality of Oak Creek, a little town in Colorado, recently took a premonitory measure in establishing *mandatory self-defense,* levying a fine of 300 dollars against any adult *not* in possession of a firearm.

[3] A. Einstein and L. Infeld, *L'Evolution des ideés en physique,* Payot, 1974.

SOVIETEXT[E]

NANCY CONDEE & VLADIMIR PADUNOV, EDITORS

Contemporary Soviet writers and artists and their Western critics contribute to an autonomous examination of that country's newly-revolutionary recent cultural and political transformations, presenting material well beyond the sedate, customary, officially approved networks of either Russian or American officialdom.

Fall, 1990 — $12 postpaid

SEMIOTEXT[E] SF

RUDY RUCKER, ROBERT ANTON WILSON & PETER LAMBORN WILSON, EDITORS

DESIGNED BY MIKE SAENZ

Writing from the nether regions of the modern science / speculative fiction universe, altered states served up on post-political platters, cyberpunkish, cybergnostic, by turns filthy, mean and angry, freakish and foul, sensuous and sexy, vile, visionary, and altogether beyond compromise. William Burroughs, J. G. Ballard, Philip José Farmer, Bruce Sterling, the editors, many more.

Now Available — $12 postpaid

A DAY IN THE LIFE
TALES FROM THE LOWER EAST SIDE
ALAN MOORE AND JOSH GOSCIAK, EDITORS

This provocative anthology of voices old and new from New York's East Village will offend those who like their literature quaint, pretty, and much too tidy to touch. Stories reflecting the turbulent mosaic of artists, ethnics, poets, junkies, barflies, radicals, mystics, street people, con men, flower children, losers, screwballs and professional eccentrics that inhabit the city's edgiest neighborhood. Allen Ginsberg, Ted Berrigan, Herbert Huncke, Lynne Tillman, Ed Sanders, Miguel Piñero, Emily XYZ, Zoe Anglesley, Jorge Cabalquinto, Cookie Mueller, Ron Kolm, and many more, with art by Seth Tobacman, Keiko Bonk, Martin Wong, and others. An Evil Eye Book. Now Available — $10 postpaid

THE LOST DIMENSION
PAUL VIRILIO

The French urban planner and cultural theorist examines aspects of post-modern society ranging from space travel to time and the physical sciences. Fall, 1990 — $12 postpaid

POPULAR REALITY
IRREVEREND DAVID CROWBAR, EDITOR

The oversized anthology of selections from the controversial — and now autodissolute— marginal magazine, the "Vital Organ of the Shimo Undeground." Graphics and text, détourned advertisements and more from Bob Black, Blaster Al Ackerman, the Irreverend Crowbar, Bob McGlynn, Hakim Bey, Celeste Oatmeal, Yael Dragwyla, tENTATIVELY a cONVENIENCE, the Wretched Dervish, and many more.
Fall, 1990 — $12 postpaid

CASSETTE MYTHOS
MAKING MUSIC AT THE MARGINS
ROBIN JAMES, EDITOR

Essays, reports, stories, and manifestoes from the real musical underground, where the medium of the tape cassette has made it possible for individuals and groups to produce and distribute their own music in their own style and for their own purposes, free of the censuring, perception-clogging nets of cash and commerce.
Fall, 1990 — $12 postpaid

COLUMBUS & OTHER CANNIBALS
THE WÉTIKO DISEASE & THE WHITE MAN
JACK D. FORBES

A noted American Indian scholar and activist examines the heritage of indigenous American cultures since the coming of Europeans in the 15th century, with a particular focus on the "wétiko disease," the White Man's fascination with the exploitation and control of nature and his fellow man.
Spring, 1991 — $12 postpaid

"GONE TO CROATAN"
ORIGINS OF AMERICAN DROPOUT CULTURE
JAMES KOEHNLINE & PETER LAMBORN WILSON, EDITORS

Studies of lost American history and the cultures of disappearance, including "tri-racial isolate" communities, the bucaneers, "white Indians," black Islamic movements, the Maroons of the Great Dismal Swamp, scandalous eugenics theories, rural "hippie" communes, and many other aspects of American autonomous cultures.
A *festschrift* in honor of historian Hugo Leaming Bey of the Moorish Science Temple.
Spring, 1991 — $12 postpaid

TROTSKYISM AND MAOISM
THEORY AND PRACTICE IN FRANCE & THE U.S.A.
A. BELDEN FIELDS

An important examination of the critical heritage
of Trotsky and Mao in two Western national
contexts, focusing on the multitudinous parties
and sects and their positions on national and
international issues, racism, sexism, party / worker
positions, gay rights, and students movements.
Charts of organizational histories.
Now Available — $12 postpaid

MODEL CHILDREN
MY SOVIET SUMMERS AT ARTEK
PAUL THOREZ

The son of long-time French Communist Party
chief Maurice Thorez recounts his post-war
childhood experiences at Artek, the prestigious
Crimean summer camp for children of the Soviet
elite, where he saw aspects of Russian political
culture rarely revealed to the West.
Photos and Maps.
Now Available — $12 postpaid

TE BWE WIN
STORIES BY AN OJIBWAY HEALER
RON GEYSHICK

By turns haunting, humorous, fantastic and powerful, stories that explore the traditional spiritual world of the Ojibway, as experienced by a healer and guide from the Neguagon Lake Indian Reservation on the border of Minnesota and Ontario. Te Bwe Win ("Truth") moves from the mysterious and eternal symbols of his people's spritual heritage to the world of snowmobiles, outboard motors and all-star wrestling on the VCR. Additional stories by filmmaker Judith Doyle.
An Impulse Edition, Summerhill Press.
Now Available — $15 postpaid

I SHOT MUSSOLINI
ELDON GARNET

A hallucinogenic novel, mysterious, challenging and violent, by the editor of the Canadian avant-garde literary magazine, Impulse. In his remarkable meditation on history, Garnet explores questions of memory and terrorism and the way in which communication manipulates truth.
An Impulse Edtion, Summerhill Press.
Now Available — $15 postpaid

AESTHETICS OF DISAPPEARANCE
PAUL VIRILIO

From infantile narcolepsy to the illusion of
movement in speed, the author of *Pure War*
and *Speed and Politics* and other works examines
the "aesthetic" of disappearance: in film,
in politics, in war, in the philosophy of
subjectivity, and elsewhere.
Now Available — $12 postpaid

CLIPPED COINS, ABUSED WORDS, AND CIVIL GOVERNMENT
JOHN LOCKE'S PHILOSOPHY OF MONEY
CONSTANTINE GEORGE CAFFENTZIS

Starting from the political crisis arising from the
"clipping" of silver currency by monetary pirates
in 17th-century England, Caffentzis opens out
into an original and very provocative critique
of John Locke's economic beliefs, his theories
of language, and his philosophy of history
and the state. Virtually all of the standard critical
work on Locke is "undone" through Caffentzis'
ampliative treatment—which also extends to
intervene in the leading debates in the
monetary theories of the present day.
Now Available — $12 postpaid